AF270549

Praise for *The Six Secrets of Change, Second Edition*

"I started reading the manuscript and could not put it down! For more than three decades, I have worked to drive systemic change in education. Michael Fullan has long guided that effort, reminding us through his 'six secrets' that true reform requires strategies that reinforce one another. His new book offers a hopeful and actionable path forward in an era of growing complexity and disruption. Drawing on what we know and have experienced, he scales it into a fresh approach to systems change—one that includes harnessing Artificial Intelligence wisely. Fullan challenges us to be critical consumers of technology rather than passive recipients. By combining the 'what' and 'why' of effective change with the essential 'how,' this book becomes a vital road map for anyone committed to shaping the future of humanity."

—Jean-Claude Brizard,
President and CEO, Digital Promise

"Few have had more widespread influence than Michael Fullan on thinking about the future of education and how we can dislodge a tenacious status quo that serves fewer and fewer. Hidden behind Fullan's pragmatic and compelling exposition of the 'six secrets' is a powerful and urgent challenge to the reader: How must I change? How can I find and help others cultivate fertile soil for understanding genuine learning and human development?"

—Peter Senge,
Senior Lecturer, Massachusetts Institute of Technology

"Few scholars have shaped global education reform more than Michael Fullan. In this new edition, he re-examines the Six Secrets of Change, showing how both change itself and our understanding of it have shifted in a complex, post-pandemic world. For policymakers, educators, and change agents, this book is indispensable for navigating education system renewal."

—**Pasi Sahlberg,**
Professor in Educational Leadership,
University of Melbourne

"*The Six Secrets of Change 2.0* is my anchor in the storm. It cuts through the illusion that meaningful change comes only from distant strategy, hierarchy, or top-down control. It grounds me where spirit work lives—close to the action, building trust and belonging, and connecting people to the purpose of our work. It steadies my practice and sharpens my focus. It reframes how I see the system itself. Hope comes from the idea that people at every level can act, learn together, and reshape the system from within. It's not naive optimism; it's grounded, disciplined hope—and this book is full of it. It leaves you not just inspired, but ready to act with greater clarity and purpose."

—**Marie-Claire Bretherton,**
Deputy CEO, Waterton Academy Trust, UK

"Michael's combination of deep wisdom and deep optimism is unparalleled. This book does far more than simply update the original six secrets—it reimagines them for an age of AI and extraordinary change. In doing so, Michael brings together his long experience of school and system change with his cutting edge work with leading experts to reimagine the role and purpose of schools. Highly recommended!"

—**Toby Greany,**
Professor of Education, University of Nottingham

"*The Six Secrets of Change 2.0* deepens Fullan's compelling argument for the necessity of transformation, the 'why.' At the same time, it provides the equally persuasive arguments about 'how' this might be achieved. He demonstrates, for example, how the six secrets can partner with AI to generate even deeper change that has specificity, precision, and timeliness; that has in his words ongoing 'proximity to practice.'"

—**Anthony Mackay,**
Board Co-Chair, National Center on Education &
the Economy, Washington DC

"Fullan deepens and extends some of the original six secret gems that he has given us continuing to provide us with practical examples of how to seek the changes we all desire. This book provides a path to 'increase the likelihood that desirable and effective change for humanity can be achieved in increasingly complex and negative circumstances.' The hidden secret that we all know is that this is people work and has to be done in collaboration, and in context. *The Six Secrets of Change 2.0* shows us how to do this, making it possible, and essential."

—**Jordan Tinney,**
Leadership Consultant, Former Superintendent,
Surrey School District, BC

"Michael Fullan has done it once again. He boils down the complexity of today to six secrets. These six secrets change the narrative from a pervasive, reactive, negative rhetoric to a guide for success for all our students and staff. It is time to step back and commit to the work ahead that he is fully articulating. As Michael says, 'with specificity without imposition.' Fullan integrates the learning in the classroom with the organizational challenges. The result is a seamless strategy for success. *The Six Secrets of Change 2.0* is an inspirational must read!"

—**Lyle Kirtman,**
President, Future Management Systems

"In *The Six Secrets of Change 2.0*, renowned educational change expert Michael Fullan provides clear and compelling guidance to leaders on how to transform systems so that educators and students can thrive. This highly readable and insightful volume unlocks the secrets for system transformation in a rapidly shifting world with economic uncertainties, the advent of AI, and other forces shaping schooling today. Engaging examples from the education sector and beyond, Fullan's book will help leaders engage their communities in creating a powerful new framework for the future."

—**Amanda Datnow,**
Acting Senior Associate Vice Chancellor, Academic Affairs; Chancellor's Associates Endowed Chair and Professor, Dept. of Education Studies, University of California San Diego

"As AI accelerates "dynamic complexity", Michael Fullan's *The Six Secrets of Change 2.0* delivers a new "systemness" framework for leaders, moving beyond shallow implementation to cultivate the deep, human-centric readiness our organizations and students truly need."

—Alex Kotran,
Co-Founder & CEO of aiedu.or

THE SIX
SECRETS
OF
CHANGE 2.0

THE SIX SECRETS OF CHANGE 2.0

What the Best Leaders Do to Help Their Organizations Survive and Thrive

Michael Fullan

JOSSEY-BASS™
A Wiley Brand

Copyright © 2026 by John Wiley & Sons, Inc. All rights reserved, including rights for text and data mining and training of artificial intelligence technologies or similar technologies.

Published by John Wiley & Sons, Inc., Hoboken, New Jersey.

No part of this publication may be reproduced, stored in a retrieval system, or transmitted in any form or by any means, electronic, mechanical, photocopying, recording, scanning, or otherwise, except as permitted under Section 107 or 108 of the 1976 United States Copyright Act, without either the prior written permission of the Publisher, or authorization through payment of the appropriate per-copy fee to the Copyright Clearance Center, Inc., 222 Rosewood Drive, Danvers, MA 01923, (978) 750-8400, fax (978) 750-4470, or on the web at www.copyright.com. Requests to the Publisher for permission should be addressed to the Permissions Department, John Wiley & Sons, Inc., 111 River Street, Hoboken, NJ 07030, (201) 748-6011, fax (201) 748-6008, or online at http://www.wiley.com/go/permission.

The manufacturer's authorized representative according to the EU General Product Safety Regulation is Wiley-VCH GmbH, Boschstr. 12, 69469 Weinheim, Germany, e-mail: Product_Safety@wiley.com.

Trademarks: Wiley and the Wiley logo are trademarks or registered trademarks of John Wiley & Sons, Inc. and/or its affiliates in the United States and other countries and may not be used without written permission. All other trademarks are the property of their respective owners. John Wiley & Sons, Inc. is not associated with any product or vendor mentioned in this book.

Limit of Liability/Disclaimer of Warranty: While the publisher and the author have used their best efforts in preparing this work, including a review of the content of the work, neither the publisher nor the author make any representations or warranties with respect to the accuracy or completeness of the contents of this work and specifically disclaim all warranties, including without limitation any implied warranties of merchantability or fitness for a particular purpose. No warranty may be created or extended by sales representatives, written sales materials, or promotional statements for this work. The fact that an organization, website, or product is referred to in this work as a citation and/or potential source of further information does not mean that the publisher and authors endorse the information or services the organization, website, or product may provide or recommendations it may make. This work is sold with the understanding that the publisher is not engaged in rendering professional services. The advice and strategies contained herein may not be suitable for your situation. You should consult with a specialist where appropriate. Further, readers should be aware that websites listed in this work may have changed or disappeared between when this work was written and when it is read. Neither the publisher nor authors shall be liable for any loss of profit or any other commercial damages, including but not limited to special, incidental, consequential, or other damages.

For general information on our other products and services or for technical support, please contact our Customer Care Department within the United States at (800) 762-2974, outside the United States at (317) 572-3993 or fax (317) 572-4002.

Wiley also publishes its books in a variety of electronic formats. Some content that appears in print may not be available in electronic formats. For more information about Wiley products, visit our website at www.wiley.com.

Library of Congress Cataloging-in-Publication Data:

Names: Fullan, Michael, author.
Title: The six secrets of change 2.0 : what the best leaders do to help
  their organizations survive and thrive / Michael Fullan.
Description: Second edition. | San Francisco : Jossey-Bass, [2026]
Identifiers: LCCN 2026002086 (print) | LCCN 2026002087 (ebook) | ISBN
  9781394382149 (paperback) | ISBN 9781394382163 (adobe pdf) | ISBN
  9781394382156 (epub)
Subjects: LCSH: Organizational change. | Communication in organizations. |
  Interpersonal communication. | Employee empowerment. | Employee
  motivation.
Classification: LCC HD58.8 .F84 2026 (print) | LCC HD58.8 (ebook)
LC record available at https://lccn.loc.gov/2026002086
LC ebook record available at https://lccn.loc.gov/2026002087

Cover Design: Wiley
Cover Image: © MirageC/Getty Images
SKY10151659_040726

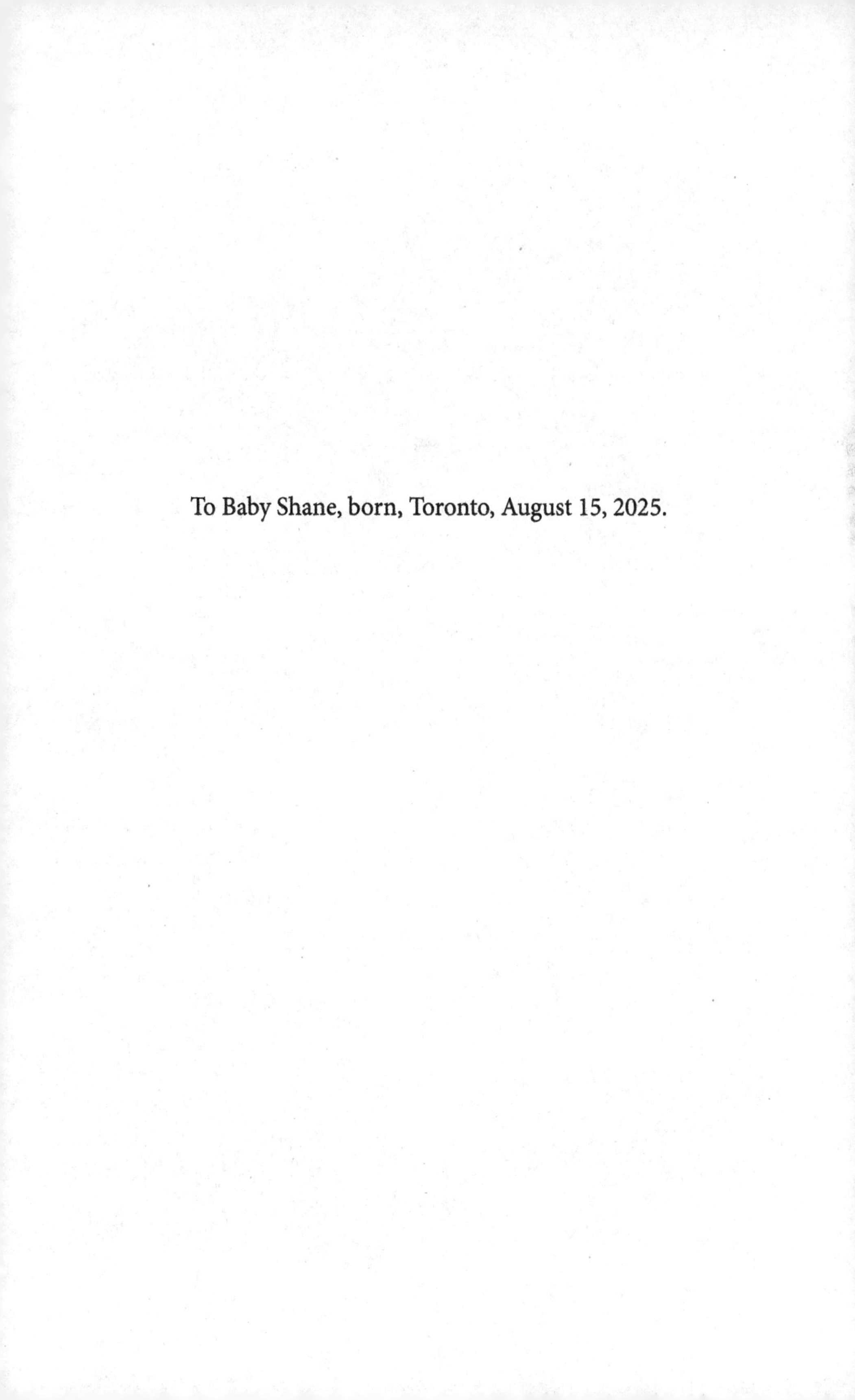

To Baby Shane, born, Toronto, August 15, 2025.

CONTENTS

FOREWORD
The Six Secrets of Change 2.0

THE SECOND EDITION OF *THE SIX SECRETS OF CHANGE* (SSC 2.0) is many things. It is certainly the Six Secrets "updated" to address the age of disruption and hyper change. Drawing on lessons from complexity in non-linear environments Fullan identifies the leadership required for each Secret and encourages us to see the Secrets as a "Set." He stresses how the six are interrelated, interacting with each other to address what he identifies as the crucial "systemness factor" (Fullan's systemness mindset).

SSC 2.0 continues the crusade to successfully generate large-scale change—deep and lasting. For the field of education this requires nothing less than the transformation of our learning systems. *SSC 2.0* provides new breakthroughs and insights to guide leaders to "help their organizations to survive and thrive" in both the public and private spheres. But *SSC 2.0* is much more.

Fullan reminds us that the leadership and management lessons identified are secrets not because there is a conspiracy to hide them from the public view but because they are often difficult to grasp in their deep meaning and challenging to appreciate and act on in combination.

"Updated" does not do justice to the insights gained from a remarkable capture of previously published work harnessed for the purpose of informing new system transformation. This second edition is demanding—as it should be. The revelation of multiple new breakthroughs requires probing at many levels with clear implications for new action.

For those who have closely followed Michael's work and who most recently have been influenced by the 2025 publication of the sixth edition of *The New Meaning of Educational Change* (NMEC), *SSC 2.0* provides a "playbook" for transformative action.

To know and understand the Six Secrets—and their interrelationship—is to enable the formation and execution of a strategy and accompanying tactics to have a better than even chance to successfully play and win "the transformation game."

In short, *SSC 2.0* deepens Fullan's compelling argument for the necessity of transformation, the "why." At the same time, it provides the equally persuasive arguments about "how" this might be achieved. He demonstrates, for example, how the Six Secrets can partner with AI to generate even deeper change that has specificity, precision, and timeliness; that has in his words ongoing "proximity to practice."

Each Secret brings both breakthrough ideas and energy to recognize and act on the complexity of our environment, to enable the lessons of change and transformation to be applied with deeper appreciation of the nuances involved—sensitive to and applicable for the diverse settings, cultures, and contexts that confront us (Fullan's contextual literacy).

Fullan reminds us that this endeavor unlocks secrets for ourselves, allowing us to create the change conditions for others. The internal dimension relates to the transformation of self, the authorizing of self. We are reminded of the fundamental challenge of how system change is related to self-change (Fullan's Spirit work, Trust and Interact).

In *SSC 2.0* there is a substantial Part 1: leading into the Six Secrets (setting the direction); Part 2: The Secrets themselves; and Part 3: the way forward arising from Secrets (the new world).

Like OECD's 2025 edition of *Trends Shaping Education* covering key trends, cross cutting themes, and futures thinking, Fullan sets the scene for *SSC 2.0* with the challenge of navigating for big risks with the probability of high payoff.

We confront mis/disinformation, climate risk, conflict and fragility, societal disruption and growing inequities. We are reminded that we need a purpose to our lives that will focus on human development, investing in our human capabilities harnessing the positive power of technology in the age of AI.

In addition to a state-of-the-art treatment of AI, Fullan pays particular attention to the insights from the sciences of learning and development and new and emerging learning sciences (transcendent thinking; embodiment science).

As fully explained in the 6th edition of the NMEC we confront the failures of decades of large-scale reform—inconvenient truths—and a shift to the essential recognition of proximity to practice, to partnerships with practitioners, to doing the work, and keeping close to the action (Fullan's Connected Autonomy and Legacy Leaders).

We desperately need to retrieve lost ground in our capacity to flourish—to solve complex problems, to exercise ethical decision-making, and to regain aesthetic awareness—to employ nuance in times of dynamic complexity.

Fullan's rallying cry is for us to take action guided by the insights within the Secrets and their dynamic connection with each other. By arming us with the Six Secrets of Change, Fullan employs the discipline of anticipation and persistence to tackle systemness change now and in the future.

SSC 2.0 inspires and motivates us to lead transformation—to be proactive in the face of inertia. To break out of being "stuck" as he calls it. We know that system shift needs to generate legitimacy from public confidence and stakeholder engagement—involving a political power shift to participative democracy, community action, and the power of networking.

Olli-Pekka Heinonen, the Director General of IBO, recently released a book with a title that echoes the Fullan imperative—*Learning as If Life Depended on It: Why We Must See the World Anew and Figure Out What Follows.*

Applying the *SSC 2.0* promises to be a powerful path to follow. In Fullan's words: "...it is a chance for humanity to regain the evolutionary potential for a remarkable future."

Anthony Mackay
Board Co-Chair, National Center on Education &
the Economy, Washington, DC.
Board Co-Chair, Learning Creates Australia, Melbourne.

PART 1
A Secret World

NUANCE MEETS DYNAMIC COMPLEXITY

THE ORIGINAL SIX SECRETS

THE BIG DECLINE

TURNING THE SYSTEM ON ITS HEAD

·PART 2·
Real Secrets Are Mysterious and Deep

·PART 3·
Systemness Change and the Future

A Secret World

Nuance Meets
Dynamic Complexity

Secrets are, by definition, elusive. You can have simple secrets, such as "who slept with whom"; or complex ones: "How in this world can any group be successful in bringing about complex change in 2026?" I am interested in the latter. How can you learn to bring about positive change that benefits yourself and others in a world where lots can go wrong? It turns out that there are certain insights that are learnable that increase the odds of causing positive change. They work with people who have differences. They help people find and foster common ground. The secrets are complex because they require understanding and enabling dynamic interaction. They work best when situations worsen because humans get sick of constant negativity.

My original *Six Secrets* was published in 2008. Ironically, as you will see they were formed when things seemed to be on the right track in some jurisdictions (Ontario, for example). Since 2008 things have been getting steadily worse as I will later document. The new secrets, amplified in the face of adversity, furnish greater insight, depth, and action guidelines for what to do now (2026) when the system has dramatically worsened.

The purpose of the new six secrets is to increase the likelihood that desirable and effective change for humanity can be achieved in increasingly complex and negative circumstances. Paradoxically as situations worsen secrets find more fertile ground. As a species humans are facing the worst series of crises that it has ever faced—certainly in the past 100 years. Join me in a quest to increase your capacity, individually and collectively to blunt negative change forces as you develop a new foundation for positive transformation. Part of our hidden power is the mobilization of the new six secrets—a phenomenon that could find more traction in bad times, than when things seem to be going okay.

All secrets worth their salt are mysterious until you master them. Da Vinci didn't "discover" the Mona Lisa. He *created* her over decades. When I published the first edition of the *Six Secrets*, I was thinking that each had hidden depth to be uncovered and mined. I wasn't thinking at the time that the six formed a *set*. I do now in this second edition. The secrets feed each other. Because the particular future we now face is intrinsically complex and bound to be non-linear, we need to take the mindset of an apprentice—learn about complexity as we go. In 2026, apprentices need to be fast learners. For that you need to place yourself in the center of some action. You can't afford to be a bystander.

In addition to updating the insights germane to each secret I have made two other changes. First, I have added details of the kind of "leadership" required for each secret in question. Such leadership applies to anyone acting with initiative—young or old, formal or informal leadership. Second, I examine more explicitly how the secrets interact with each other. What I call the "systemness" factor. It turns out that the secrets had certain depth and resonance with each other that I hadn't realized at the time. *SSC 2.0* will give you some guidance and action examples to be on the right track. In this complex non-linear world, all of us need to be to some extent explorers. If you want to survive and thrive, be a purposeful learner.

Keeping close to the action these days is not for the faint hearted. If equipped with the right secrets, however, it is worth the effort because allowing a dysfunctional status quo to unfold is more dangerous to most of us in both the short and long runs. I will use a new paradigm or model that turns the system on its head. Instead of thinking of "top" (policy), "middle" (districts, regions), and "local" (schools and communities) I will reverse the thinking to "develop the bottom," "strengthen the middle," and "intrigue the top." As such they form a *system* for which I have used a new term: "systemness"—the degree to which the elements are interdependent. When participants become "aware" that they are part and parcel of a system in action, their insights and commitment increase. If there is one change finding that stands out in this century it is that *interaction effects* are the dominant force for both good and bad change. Systemness deliberately fosters mutual awareness so that people can learn what works best relative to a given goal. I will spell out and develop this crucial new phenomenon—the subjective awareness of the system—as we proceed through the six secrets.

Secrets help people grasp nuance—a subtle distinction in meaning or a deeper understanding of complex interactions. I wrote a book that showed that "nuance" was what distinguished effective from ineffective leaders (Fullan, 2019). The Six Secrets as a set represents *system nuance*. Anyone can learn them through immersive action and reflection, especially if you do so with others. Most changes that improve your local situation did not come from someone getting approval. A lot of the best changes that derive from the secrets do not require permission. Likewise, many best ideas are emerging in various places. The problem is that they just don't circulate in our segmented and divisive society. This book addresses this very issue—how to uncover, spread, use, and refine the secrets in action.

All six secrets come from action in the first place. Our team has been immersed in applied system change, especially in the past five years. As such we have been uncovering new insights. We do this through partnership with an array of practitioners, students included of course, that brings us closer to the secret world of best practice under the most challenging circumstances that the education world has ever faced. A new finding is that "proximity to practice" is essential. When things get complex leadership has to become more dispersed, close to day-to-day action. We find that our most powerful insights come from working closely with practitioners, including students. Ongoing proximity yields troves of practical insights.

The second and related finding is that "specificity without imposition" (or if you like precision without prescription) must prevail. People won't share if they are being prematurely judged. People have to try things in order to discover and develop best insights. Thus, transparency and co-development go hand in hand. We will find that new success often consists of the discovery of patterns that emerge through actions we take in response to the changing agenda of issues we identify in working with practitioners.

There is still a lot of truth to be found in the 2008 SSC book, but it is no longer adequate to explain let alone cause success in current society. In 2025, in the latest edition of *The New Meaning of Educational Change* (Fullan, 2025, 6th Edition) I reviewed the history of large-scale system reform in education from around the world from 1965 to the present. I concluded that as of 2025 no country, no large-scale system had been successful by the end of the 60-year period that I examined. One discovery I made in retrospect was that the period covering 2008–2016 was a kind of "while we were sleeping" phenomenon. Without realizing it we went backward. We then lost even more ground in the helter-skelter conditions in the ensuing decade 2017 to the present including COVID-19 and its aftermath.

Where does one "re-start" in 2026? Today we are seeking success amidst failure and turmoil. This makes the secrets of success less obvious (and all the more important). Fortunately, our method of system learning is in the tradition of Leonardo da Vinci and Kurt Lewin. The former is a champion of "nuance." If you want to find out how something works, and could work better, get inside it and see what makes it tick for better or worse. Find places where it works and start refining forward (see Walter Isaacson's (2017) brilliant biography on Leonardo da Vinci). My other apprenticeship was via Kurt Lewin: "If you want to understand something, try changing it." And "there is nothing so practical as good theory," and our own "there is nothing so theoretical as good practice." In short, we base our secrets on the experience of working closely and daily with practitioners. Pulling out the nuances of experienced change—success and failure—is the essence of the current book.

As my earlier optimism failed to pan out our team sought "new secrets" through investigative case studies of whole systems (we don't work with individual schools in isolation). We just finished two publications on this work that form sources of inspiration and evidence that furnish new insights about the "secrets" of change. The new ideas are compatible with the original six but more precise and fit for the times (Barry, Matsuda, & Fullan, in press; Fine, Rincón-Gallardo, & Fullan, in press). Overall, I don't think there is any doubt that at this point we are losing ground relative to sorting out what can only be called a dubious and dangerous future for present day humanity.

Since 1993 when I published *Change Forces* I have incorporated "chaos theory" into our collective work. In particular "dynamic complexity" has informed our analysis, and more importantly has guided our solutions. "Dynamic complexity" refers to phenomena influenced by many unpredictable factors. The search for insightful secrets involves uncovering and discovering underlying solutions that could bring success under increasingly entangled scenarios. Interaction effects of two or more variables can be especially instructive.

Complexity theorist Ralph Stacey put it this way:

"The long-term future . . . is completely unknown because the links between specific actions and specific outcomes become lost in the detail of what happens . . . When we operate in a chaotic system, it follows that successful human organizations cannot be the realization of some shared intention formed well ahead of action. Instead, success has to be the discovery of patterns that emerge through actions we take in response to the changing agenda of issues we identify" (Stacey, 1992, p. 124; see also Fullan, 1993, *Change Forces*).

The secrets won't be of full use until you understand the subtleties of each one in action and interaction. My advice is to soak up the meaning of the secrets in Part 2. I will then pull them together in action in Part 3, including the mysterious role of Artificial Intelligence.

The Original Six Secrets

The Big Decline

Turning the System on Its Head

The New Six Secrets

In Search of a Better Future

Systemness in Action

The Future

The Original Six Secrets

We can start with the secrets as originally identified, quoted directly below (Fullan, 2008). In Part 2 I will update them as they fit present circumstances in 2026.

1. Love your employees.

    If you build your organization by focusing on your customers without making the same careful commitment to your employees, you won't succeed for long. And we have all seen the opposite: the organization that seems to run for the benefit of the employees, with the customer perceived as an intrusion. Neither will do. I will provide powerful evidence that investing in your employees in the right way can be enormously profitable. The key is in enabling employees to learn continuously and to find meaning in their work and in their relationship to coworkers and to the company as a whole. As we will see in this new edition (almost two decades later), this secret has become more important. The biggest motivator for many young people in job seeking is finding meaning and purpose in their work. (Note: I am using the term employees metaphorically to include all members of the organization. Students and teachers are "employees" in this sense.)

2. Connect peers with purpose.

All large-scale reform in the public or private sector faces what I call the too tight–too loose dilemma. If you want large-scale reform, you had better focus and tighten the requirements; but if you go too far, people feel constrained, and rebel. At the same time, local people need to be empowered. But if you devolve power and resources to local entities—the "let a thousand flowers bloom" approach—you get uneven results. (A thousand flowers do not in fact bloom, and those that do are not perennial!) I will show, with plenty of concrete examples, that the solution to this dilemma can be helped from the top, but not directly. It comes from leaders who embed strategies that foster continuous and purposeful peer interaction. The social glue of simultaneously tight-loose systems will stick, not when rank-and-file workers fall in love with the hierarchy—those in charge at the top—but rather when they fall in love with their peers, and the nature of their work together. The job of leaders is to provide good direction while pursuing its implementation through purposeful peer interaction and learning in relation to results.

3. Capacity building prevails.

Capacity building entails leaders investing in the development of individual and collaborative efficacy of a whole group or system to accomplish significant improvements. In particular, capacity consists of new competencies, new resources (time, ideas, expertise), and new motivation. Many theories of action use fear and punitive accountability.

I will maintain that this gets at best short-term and fleeting results. Bullying backfires when it comes to complex change. The opposite of such approaches—non-judgmentalism— doesn't mean that you avoid identifying things as effective or ineffective. Rather it means that you do not do so pejoratively. Put another way, there are better ways to instill fear and motivation than through negative judgment—for example, by combining transparency and peer interaction. Pejorative judgments have their place, as when someone is abusive or engaged in criminal and fraudulent acts, but as motivators they need to be used sparingly. The main gains will come from the six secrets in concert, none of which contains blatant judgmentalism.

4. Learning is the work.

One of my Australian colleagues wrote a paper with the wonderful title "Professional Development: A Great Way to Avoid Change" (Cole, 2004). In other words, there is far too much going to workshops, taking short courses, and the like, and far too little learning while doing the work. Learning external to the job can represent a useful input, but if it is not in balance and in concert with learning in the setting in which you work, the learning will end up being superficial. I will present evidence that effective organizations see working and learning to work better as one and the same. Most real change occurs on the job or it doesn't occur at all.

5. Transparency rules.

By transparency I mean clear and continuous display of results, and direct access to practice (what is being done to get the results). Transparency can be abused, such as when results are used punitively, but there is no way that continuous improvement can occur without continual transparency fueled by good data. When this secret is implemented in combination with the other five, the gains far outweigh the costs. Besides, transparency is here to stay in the flat world of the 21st century. When transparency is consistently evident, it can create an aura of "positive pressure"—pressure that is experienced as fair and reasonable, pressure that is actionable in that it points to solutions, and pressure that ultimately is inescapable.

6. Systems learn.

Systems can learn on a continuous basis. The synergistic result of the previous five secrets in action is tantamount to a system that learns from itself. Two dominant change forces are unleashed and constantly cultivated: knowledge and commitment. People learn new things all the time, and their sense of meaning and their motivation are continually stimulated and deepened. As we shall see, learning also means being humble in the face of complexity.

At that time—2008—I felt confident that we were on the right track. As it turned out there were hidden factors at work that have taken their toll. The original six secrets are no longer up to the challenge. In addition, we need powerful new understanding of the secrets for the next phase. Truth, for example, is hard to come by in 2026. Thus, we need to design change strategies in a way that participants find new insights. This is the focus of the rest of the book.

The Original Six Secrets

The Big Decline

Turning the System on Its Head

The New Six Secrets

In Search of a Better Future

Systemness in Action

The Future

The Big Decline

*B*efore we turn to the revised *Six Secrets*, we need to examine the state of play for what has become a radically multifaceted disruption in the almost 20 years since SSC 2008. Altogether there have been four massive disruptions in this time frame: deepening economic inequality, growing loss of purpose in schools and public education, Covid, and Artificial Intelligence.

Deepening Economic Inequality

*O*ne set of developments that was initially hidden is "galloping" (there is no more accurate word for it) worldwide financial inequality. It began quietly starting just after the recession in 2008 (actually earlier but 2008 suits my main point). This deadly trend was eventually documented with a bang when a group of women economists examined the facts: Marianne Mazzucato (2018, 2021), Helen Boushey (2019), and Kate Raworth (2017) exposed what can only be called galloping inequality between the small percentage of the haves and the growing number of have nots. We are now belatedly familiar with these developments (every now and then I feed a key question to AI—in this case, Gemini—to give the reader a sense of how it works, and I will always acknowledge it when I do so). Here so from Gemini:

- In recent decades, global financial inequality has grown significantly, even as economic growth has continued. This trend, which was initially less visible, has since become a major area of study for economists.

- **Growing Wealth Gap:** While GDP has risen, a dispro-portionate share of that growth has been captured by a small percentage of the population.
  - Between 1975 and 2017, the U.S. real GDP tripled from $5.9 trillion to $17.29 trillion.

During the same period, the share of total wealth held by the richest 1% expanded from 9.4% to 22.6%.

- **Extreme Wealth Concentration:** The concentration of wealth at the very top has led to stark comparisons.
  - In 2015, the combined wealth of the 62 richest people in the world was equivalent to that of the poorest 3.5 billion people. A decade later, 2025, the gap is much worse.

- **Persistent Trends:** Subsequent analysis shows these trends have worsened. According to an Oxfam report, global billionaire wealth grew by $2.8 trillion in 2024 alone, an increase of about $7.9 billion per day.

- **Impact on Society:** This level of inequality has far-reaching effects on social and economic well-being, as well as political stability. It is linked to issues such as:
  - **Limited Social Mobility:** Children of the wealthiest parents are significantly more likely to remain in the top wealth brackets.
  - **Increased Debt:** The rising cost of living for working and middle-class citizens often leads to increased household debt.
  - **Economic Distortion:** Large concentrations of wealth may not be invested in ways that benefit the broader economy, as capital is often directed toward speculative or monopolistic practices rather than productive investments.

- These developments highlight how a focus on economic growth alone, measured by GDP, can obscure underlying issues of wealth distribution and its impact on the majority of the population. Oxfam International (2025) reports that billionaire wealth "surged by $2 trillion in 2024, three times faster than the year before, while the number of people living in poverty had barely changed since 1980" (Gemini generated).

A second powerful phenomenon, decidedly so after 2010 is that public education increasingly lost its sense of purpose. Public education, which badly needed improvement, got notably worse as more and more students found schools wanting as they moved up the grades. Heather Malin (2018) Director of Research of the "Stanford University Center on Excellence" found that by the time students reached grade 11 only about 24% of senior high school students "have identified and are pursuing a purpose for life" (p. 1).

Recent research by the Brookings Institute sheds further light on these trends. In *The Disengaged Teen*, Jenny Anderson and Rebecca Winthrop concluded that a shocking majority of teens (at least two-thirds) are disengaged from schools, simultaneously bored and overwhelmed. This pronounced trend is feeding an alarming mental health crisis. As kids get older and more independent, parents often feel powerless to help. Anderson and Winthrop (2025) report that only "30 percent of students between third and twelfth grade say that what they learn in schools feels connected to their life outside the classroom" (p. xiii). Students have been even less engaged since Covid. We will take up the solution later: greater relevance and applicability of learning to the society in which students live with an increasing involvement in finding purpose in today's troublesome world.

Anderson and Winthrop's analyses in the wake of the pandemic reveal stark declines in student engagement, academic achievement, and overall well-being. The Brookings reports documented that chronic absenteeism soared, particularly among marginalized students, and that learning losses in mathematics and reading among other things persisted with no end in sight. The erosion of students' sense of belonging and purpose was not merely anecdotal. It became more and more pronounced as the predominant pattern. Anderson and Winthrop highlighted that traditional schooling structures were failing to adapt to the shifting realities and needs of learners. These findings echoed the growing chorus of voices challenging the efficacy of the current system and underscored the urgency of systemic transformation.

Harvard Professor Richard Elmore, a stalwart of promoting student and teacher learning over the past four decades, gave a lengthy Podcast interview shortly before he died in 2021 in which he concluded that "Schools are obsolete. I don't think that people are going to stand for it! They're just going to walk away" (January 2021). Indeed, this is exactly what students and teachers are doing.

The third calamity was Covid—recognized officially in March 2020. It did not directly *cause* schools to decline. It mainly took off the roof, so to speak, and exposed the lack of vitality in schools becoming obvious for all to see. It became easier and more normal not to go to school on any given day. By now—2026—it is likely that only about 20% of students at most find school worthwhile.

The fourth and final factor is Artificial Intelligence (AI) including Artificial "Generative" Intelligence (AGI), and Artificial "General" Intelligence—sometimes called Superintelligence (see attached box).

Box: The Forms of Artificial Intelligence (see Schmidt & Xu, 2025)

Machine or Artificial Intelligence (AI) refers to the capacity of a machine to simulate human-like cognitive functioning such as reasoning problem-solving creativity. It is the quest to build a machine more intelligent than ourselves. AI literally seemed to come "out of the woodwork" on November 30, 2022, when ChatGPT was released as the first Artificial "Generative" Intelligence (AGI). Beyond AI "Generative"

(Continued)

(*Continued*)

is AI "General" which seeks to build intelligence that surpasses humans including the possibility of operating beyond the control of humans (see the discussion in Part 3 where I will show that AI presents both a massive threat and a unique opportunity relative to the future of humankind).

I would suggest that the reader stock up first on their "worry list" about AI by reading Karen Hao, *Empire of AI: Inside the Reckless Race of Total Domination* (2025), and Fei Fei Li's (2023) fascinating autobiography as she grew up helping to develop AI in the 2010s (in the decade I have called "while we were sleeping").

So here we are in 2026. School systems and society do not work for the majority of the population. I wouldn't say we have bottomed out, but we are now closer than at any point in the past 75 years. It is time to go "secret seeking" once more. In complex times a system secret does not fully reveal itself by being described or observed on the surface. The best analogy is asking a Nonna, the famous Italian grandmother, for her recipe. If you are lucky enough to get the recipe, you will not be much further ahead if you just follow it step by step. There are too many nuances, not to mention a few items or steps that may have been left out. In any case a complex recipe for a complex product has too many subtleties to replicate. You have to get a feel for effective change, work with it, refine and test it further, and use it under different circumstances. Unlike Nonnas, you have to invite "users" to help refine future versions under different circumstances.

In our case, 60 or more years of experience tells us mainly one thing: top-down doesn't work. Here we need Thomas Kuhn (1962) who wrote a pioneering book called *The Structure of Scientific Revolutions*. Kuhn focused on "paradigms," which are principles that govern modes, models, and related structures of thinking and action. Kuhn states that one requirement for shifting paradigms is that the status quo model is patently not working.

Another pioneer of social science is Niccolò Machiavelli (1992/1532) who found that in instances of potential dissatisfaction with the current system, those in power naturally prefer the status quo, while those against it are not fully committed to a new form of government that they have not experienced, and maybe cannot imagine. And even if opposition to a given government results in a change, it doesn't mean that the new system will be better than the one it replaces.

In the current situation—widespread dissatisfaction with the status quo, "the secret question" is how do get rid of the old and usher in a successful replacement. The challenge, as we put it in our recent book: *Whole Schools Whole Systems* (Fine, Rincón-Gallardo, & Fullan, in press), is how to unyoke schools from the age-old system of delivering knowledge accompanied by a narrow testing regime (as it turns out "at the expense of student interest"). Such a system is so embedded in our history of schools is that it has been called "the old grammar of schooling" (the organization and culture of schooling that has been around for the past 175 or more years, see Tyack & Cuban, 1997).

We now have enough studies to show that the old system does not, cannot work. The solution consists of "unseating the old structure and culture of the system" for a new one that is effective at the new learning. The starting point for me is to notionally "turn the existing system in its head" in the service of new learning. To develop the new system, we need to capture and show it in action including its specificity, and its corresponding efficacy. I am reminded of Sir Ken Robinson's wonderful vignette. He was in a classroom observing a student during art class. He noticed a six-year-old girl drawing at the back. The teacher asked her: "what are you drawing?" The girl said, "I am drawing a picture of god," to which the teacher said, "No one knows what god looks like." The girl replied, "They will in a moment" (YouTube, TED Jan 7, 2007). This is how I feel about the early versions we have of "turning the system on its head." In our case when I say the secret is to turn the system on its head, the reader may well say "no one knows what it looks like." My reply of course is "they will in a moment."

The Original Six Secrets

The Big Decline

Turning the System on Its Head

The New Six Secrets

In Search of a Better Future

Systemness in Action

The Future

Turning the System on Its Head

ere we get into a new solution to the old problem of system change. It involves recalibrating the roles of the "local level" (schools and community), the middle (school districts and regions), and "the top" (policy). It will perhaps turn out to be an interim solution to a transformed system in the future, but we don't have time or the conditions to design a new system from scratch. My proposal is a solution that allows us to get started right away (in fact we and others are doing just that). The new *Six Secrets 2.0* will enable this new journey.

We have made a radical change in how we approach system change per se. Attempts to change school systems have had a long history of failure (see Fullan, 2025). For six decades, this tradition has regarded systemic change as originating from leadership at the top, yet it has achieved limited tangible outcomes. By contrast, over the past five years we have discovered that it is more powerful to see the "bottom" (schools and communities) as the focus of establishing new directions, sometimes working laterally with other local entities. The role of the middle (districts or regional entities)

Figure 3.1: System Change: A New Approach
(Fullan & Quinn, 2024)

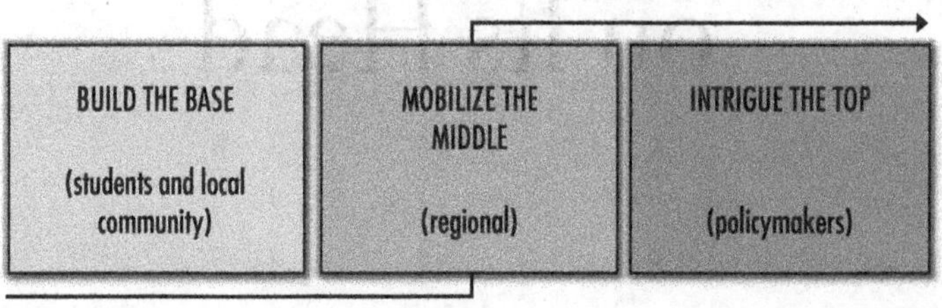

then is to help develop and support the development of the school and community level. We have deliberately challenged the top "to be intrigued" by emerging successful efforts at the other two levels (Figure 3.1). Much more about this later as the Six Secrets 2.0 has a new role to play in this new paradigm.

Thus I have set the new table differently: build the base (for example, capacity building), mobilize the middle (district or region), and (somewhat playfully) intrigue the top (policy level). Remember this is not just a theoretical model (although it is that). It is also one that we are attempting to work out in practice with incumbents at each of the levels: students, teachers, parents, principals at the base; districts and regional entities at the middle; and policy and political people at the top. I will give examples at each of these levels throughout this book. For example, we help people at the local level take action—especially collective action. We support those at the middle to build relationships within their level, and downward. The biggest problem is the third level, which I have expressed as "intrigue the top." We have several examples in our two books of what this looks like in the early stages (Berry, Matsuda, & Fullan, in press; Fine et al., in press). We will draw on this new evidence in the course of this book. I predict a growing interest at all levels, including the top, as to the operational meaning of the top "becoming intrigued" by new methods to partner with the other two levels.

We have also developed a concept that has heaps of new meaning—systemness: "one's awareness, commitment, and action to change one's level from within: intra-level (bottom, middle, or top), while engaging the other two levels. Whole systems (and all roles therein) are engaged in transforming the structures and cultures within and across levels."

Later in this book I will provide a case example of how we have applied this model: "Turning systemness on its head," in Anaheim Union High School District (AUHSD) in California—a high poverty, diverse district with 26,000 students and 20 schools. I'll later demonstrate how this new system works, noting that each system must develop its own customized version (although the effective versions have much in common).

In 2014, I wrote a book on the Principalship titled: *The Principal: Three Keys for Maximizing Impact.* The three keys were: leading learning, being a district and system player, and becoming a change agent. It was a very popular book. The problem was that I had failed to appreciate that the upper layers (above the individual school) were trying to micro-manage the school through the principal. Principals were given greater autonomy but only insofar as they delivered strong accountability on a narrow agenda. I had unwittingly set them up for continued failure (because the assignment was impossible).

I caught up to the problem and with good directional advice in *The Principal 2.0* (2023). Here I had developed a better solution to the system dilemma of where to start. In terms of "secrets" I had figured out (thanks also to my colleague, Lyle Kirtman, 2025) that focusing on outcomes and following rules *decreases* results. As I put it, "large-scale compliance diktats minimize impact—the opposite of what is intended" (p. 30). Sticking with large-scale change the "mega" system secret is that: "the hierarchy cannot *cause* success from a distance." Rather, "the principal's main job is to develop the *internal system* at the school and community levels while sorting out external demands and opportunities" (Fullan, 2023, p. 31, italics in original).

I got this insight because I continued to seek out successful school principals around the world delving into how they did this against the odds. I featured vignettes of eight different principals in four different countries in the 2023 book. Such forays enabled me to capture new "specificity" from practitioners who are discovering new powerful "nuances" that end up leading to breakthrough ideas. The following is one of my favorite examples of bottom-up change, where the principal literally led "building the base" for the so-called bottom to become an effective change agent.

We still need to work on building the relationship with the next level (the middle), which I will take up later was we develop the whole model.

Marie-Claire Bretherton from Northeast England. Fundamental Change Against the odds:

Principal Vignette

Marie-Clare Bretherton, Lincolnshire, England

Adapted from *Principal 2.0: Three Keys to Maximizing Impact*
Michael Fullan

Benjamin Adlard Primary School serves a highly deprived area in Lincolnshire about 150 miles north of London. Nearly 70% of the pupils are eligible for free school meals; poverty levels are in the bottom 10% nationally; 30% of the pupils have special needs requiring significant additional support; and the school is close to the bottom of the performance tables in the country. Bretherton, coming from a successful school in the region, took over in December 2014. She observed, "I know what I am doing in my own school that works, but I knew that it was never going to be completely translatable to Benjamin Adlard. The context was different, the staff was different, and although the mission and values were the same, the approach needed to be different. I knew a linear strategy wouldn't work."

The only staff change Bretherton made was to hire an assistant principal (Sam Coy) to help her. Here is what she did at the very beginning:

I interviewed every single member of staff, from cleaner to deputy head, just asking them everything they could tell me about the school and its history. There were so many challenges, they said. They said to me, whatever you think you know, it is not going to work here, we've tried everything. These children just aren't capable of succeeding in school; the challenges they face in life are just too big. I kept saying there is some good stuff here. At my first staff meeting I said you may think I am going to come in and sack you all.

That's not what I am going to do. All I ask is that you turn up every day and that you are willing to learn and that's all I need from you; we'll do it together. That was very counter-cultural and a big gamble. You know we didn't lose anybody. All of them stayed. I think the big challenge was the school had been isolated and the teachers within it had been isolated, too. They had no sense of connection with each other, or with schools in the local area.

My rhetoric was "we will do this together." I'm not going to come in as a leader and work in isolation with each of you. We're in this as a team so we've got to bring a kind of challenge to one another and support to one another. There was quite a bit of messaging, and there were times, honestly, that I really didn't know if I actually believed it was possible. But I gave myself a pep talk every day. It took me 20 minutes to drive from my house to the school. Every single day I would rehearse to myself about the school. So you know if you rehearse the positive, you rehearse the possible, you rehearse the vision, and it helps you that there is hope, because I knew that if I didn't do that once I arrived at school, it would only take about 10 minutes before I would be overwhelmed with hopelessness.

Sam and I had a policy. For the first eight weeks we would not give any negative feedback. We literally went on a mission to find anything that we could possibly observe that was good. We knew that as soon as we came in with a hard message pointing out where things were far from good, it would have killed any sense of optimism. We needed to build a sense that there was hope. We had to gently coach, encourage, and nourish, and build a relationship with the team so that in time we would be able to give some really specific and clear feedback about what needed to improve, but needed a relational basis on which to do it, and we needed them to know that they had strengths to build on.

As Marie-Claire and Sam built relationships, they gradually shifted to capacity building:

> There was a lot of skilling-up of the workforce, first of all in managing pupils, keeping pupils in class, and creating a culture where pupils' emotional and social needs were met. Sam and I felt we needed to do that first because if we pitched curriculum, pedagogy, and assessment first before teachers felt confident enough to manage the room, they were going to get lost. That was difficult because the accountability pressure from OFSTED was very much demanding we sort out teaching first. Once teachers felt that [they] could keep pupils in class we moved onto curriculum and instruction.
>
> We had to be very careful in terms of who we brought in, making sure that they came in with servant-hearted humility, competence and expertise, definite skills around coaching, and with the aim of building in school capacity. We did a lot of personalizing our approach to each teacher. We focused on which teachers were going to be our quick wins, who could learn quickly and raise the bar about what's possible. I think that some of the teachers who had been in the school the longest were the most difficult to get on board initially, although they became the strongest and most loyal colleagues. At the beginning there was a significant level of cynicism.
>
> One teacher, who had actually some strong areas of practice, was particularly reluctant to work with others within the school or outside the school. He was very competent with the children and how to manage them, but he was also a maverick at times. We used a tool that we created called "teacher tracker" with each teacher to identify and monitor specific

teacher competencies in terms of instruction and behavior management. Sam and I spent a lot of time in classrooms examining the trends.

The turning point for him was when we said, okay, we'd like you to go and work with the class teacher in year five because you're really strong in competency A, B, and C, and she's got D nailed. Work together. I think he realized that he had something specific to teach someone else, but also something very specific that he could use to refine his own practice further. This also gave them a clear focus. That relationship really began to transform both of them. They were observing each other teach. They were planning stuff together, marking work together, and assessing pupil progress together. They sat eyeball to eyeball and began to really digest their practice.

My big message is that it takes an alliance to improve a school. In the work of the alliance you see the power of the network, the power of peer review, the power of student voice, and the power of collective responsibility. One of the things we did was to invite pupils from other schools to come in and do a pupil—peer review, to come into the school and tell us what they thought we were missing. Among other things students told us: "Your library is full of books for girls. Where are your books for boys? Your playground is boring. It is all concrete. Where is the grass? Where is the green?" So, we brought in students from other schools to work with our students to talk about how they would make our school better, really getting into the detail."

The OFSTED (English assessment system of inspection) came in June 2016—one-and-a-half years after Bretherton started. They presented their report to me, which I then shared with the whole staff.

Oh, it was the most incredible moment of my life. It really was. We answered the question: it was possible to restore and redeem a school without sweeping it out.

So when I got the chance to tell the staff, I took them to the staff room. Everyone was standing around with bated breath. I did a bit of a preamble and then just said, "I didn't need somebody from outside to come and tell me that this is a good school and that you are really good at what you do, but I can now officially tell you that you are good—you are a good school!"

Teachers fell to their knees and wept tears of joy. Some staff described it as a life-changing moment. One teacher in particular said they felt like they could now hold their head up high and talk proudly about who they are and where they work, for the first time in their career.

Here was a school that had been stuck for many years in a sea of hopelessness. It took a special kind of leadership to lead the school out of what anyone familiar with the community would have said was a hopeless proposition. This case puts a new light on the question of school turnaround. This is not a matter of raising academic performance (although it did that). Rather, it was, and there is no other way to put it, *spirit work in action that changes the sense of humanity, life chances, and orientation to the world of students, teachers, parents, and community members.* The staff did not know what they didn't know. After experiencing a different approach under guided participatory leadership, they adopted and pursued a new method that changed their work environment as well as the experiences of the children and parents they served.

I asked Bretherton what she had learned about leadership:

> Putting the school improvement bit to one side, it was actually the transformation of humanity that really meant something to me in the school. It restored professional confidence. It's given them life. It's given them hope. It's given them purpose. The school is now oversubscribed. We've got people wanting to come and work here. We've just announced that the school has won the silver award in the Pearson Teaching Awards in the category "School of the Year—Making a Difference" for its work to Transform the Community. I think I've probably underestimated in the past the power of your own sense of vision and hope, and your own mental discipline, and your own belief. That for me was a massive learning curve. Just being able to conjure up in yourself optimism and hope where you are in the face of somebody who tells you or something tells you that it's not possible. What I learned is about the leadership of humanity. It changes the lives of staff, pupils, and parents. It opened my eyes to the role of a leader in the community. I was absolutely terrified by the challenge. I had no idea I could do this. I had no clue. But I believe I've got enough in me to learn how to do it if I go into it with the right kind of attitude.

What we see in *The Principal 2.0* is that successful school principals are "blunting" or "end running" a less than effective hierarchy. They do this in order to focus full developmental attention on the system at hand. In the eventual successful system cases (which I will introduce throughout this book) the role of the principal is indeed to build the "local system"—students, teachers, parents, community. The district's role in turn is to help schools become this good and to enable them to learn from peers across and beyond the district. Eventually these examples have lessons for the middle and the top.

As we work with the new secrets throughout this book, I will take the idea of building the bottom and strengthening the middle further. The overall concept that we need is: "turn the system on its head" in order to build success from within schools, within districts, across districts, and eventually link policy and whole system learning (see Figure 3.2).

Instead of thinking that district leaders come and go—the more things change the more they remain the same—what if we became proactive about: "building the bottom, strengthening the middle, and intriguing the top"

Figure 3.2: Systemness on Its Head (Fullan & Quinn, 2024)

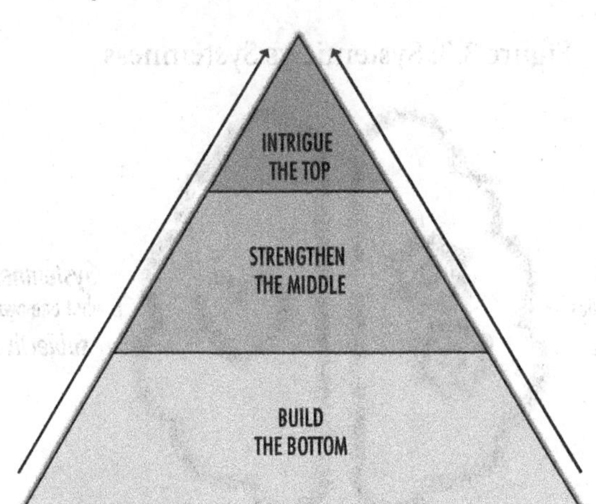

As we move to greater systemness the concept itself is coming to have greater "subjective" meaning for all participants. We are finding that people at all three levels (students, teachers, parents/community, district leaders, and even system leaders) are coming to have more of a subjective understanding of the concept of "systemness"—seeing themselves and others as part of a three-level system. They begin to see their peers (within their level) as facing many of the same issues—even thinking about others occupying roles at other levels. The more that people articulate their intra-role issues the more they can work on systemness within their roles. When districts and even policymakers enter the fray, the more we see systemness itself develop across the whole system (see Figure 3.3).

The crucial strategic point is that the reverse diagram: bottom, middle, top—functions by involving the bottom and middle early and directly *increases* the participation of local participants (teachers, students, principals, parents, and community). As I will take up in Part 3 this strengthens the "specificity" of ideas,

Figure 3.3: Systemic vs Systemness

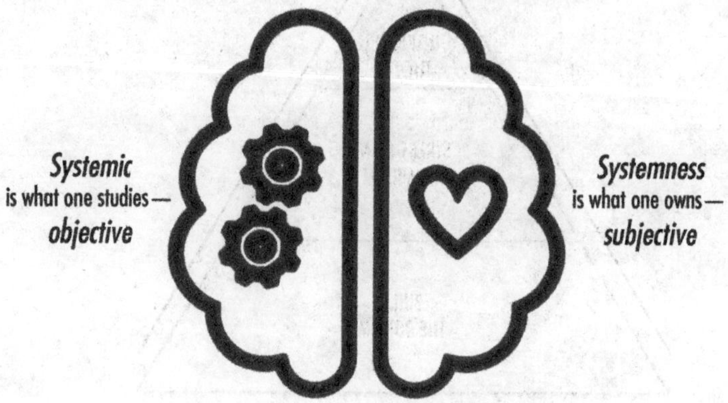

and the early participation of those who are at the heart of implementation. Part of the new paradigm is that such systems need to learn from each other. Such lateral learning strengthens both their capacity to progress (individually and in relation to each other). We are now at the stage of how best to relate to the top. Intrigue the top seems to be a good place to start.

This new system work, which is at its early stages, faces enormous challenges as the current system is in disarray. Ironically this may be the very time to formulate a new model as there is much ambiguity and disagreement about what to do. To this end, in the course of the next chapters, I revisit the *Six Secrets*. We need the "secrets"—updated with even more specificity—more than ever. I will develop them and refine the secrets anew—seeing how they can become a new secret power as a set. At the same time, I will explicitly identify the leadership skills accompanying each secret in question. Humans are more nuanced than any species. I can't claim that this book will help the reader save the world. But it should enable you to improve your learning, and your work. It should place you personally in the vanguard of future system work.

So far, the 21st century has been a flop when it comes to education. Did you know that education performance has declined across all OECD countries ever since it started to measure literacy, numeracy, and science (the so-called PISA scores) in the year 2000? Now in the midst of world turmoil is a perfect time to revisit system transformation in education.

One of our change maxims applies here: "Go slow to go fast." In dynamic and dangerous times, the "go slow" can be comparatively brief. After all we have been living with the current increasingly disruptive period for at least a decade. The new "secrets" are action oriented. We can use them as a means of simultaneously "understanding and taking action" (Kurt Lewin's "if you want to understand a system 'try changing it'"). Join us in figuring out what the new paradigm shift would look like in practice.

Using the new version of the secrets will tip the odds toward success.

Stuck

As we take stock in early 2026, the current world and almost any system around the globe seems *stuck*. At least in earlier decades many systems had plans and strategies for improvement (I reviewed this situation from 1965 to the present in *The New Meaning of Educational Change, 6th Edition*, 2025). Now I can accurately say that the world has ground to a halt or worse. Anxiety and alienation are widespread. People at all levels—students to politicians—seem stymied about what to do. Bewildered, beguiled, bedeviled—choose your state of distraction, or destruction. We are in a word *stuck*—in stagnated or in reverse. The vast majority of people—young or old—do not know what to do. Use almost any negative statistic you can find—death rates, stress, breakdown, relationships with others; they all display markedly negative trajectories. The majority of us literally *do not know what to do!*

In this final section of Part 1, I want to underscore current reality as we set the direction for Part 2 where I identify the new Six Secrets as the way forward.

How is this for a start: Marc Dunkelman's (2025) *Why Nothing Works* traces the history of policy reform in the United States over the last 100 years. Over almost 400 pages he cites chapter and verse of examples of proposed reforms, whether from the left or the right that have been stymied on the way to implementation. Dunkelman marshals example after example of progressive reforms over the decades and concludes: "Because government has failed in *all* these realms—because confidence in public authority has waned over the years—progressives have found it increasingly difficult to make a case for themselves" (p. 20).

Of course, this is as much a function of endemic prejudice and inequality as anything, but this is the point. You can't change these qualities through top-down action. It may help a little, but it won't render the solution. Dunkelman gets closer to our own resolution when he states: "Rather than tear our hair out over *their* plans [policymakers at the top] we need to train more of our attention on our own ideas, our own impulses, our own narrative" (p. 23, italics in original). This by the way is Six Secrets territory. The lesson is don't trust the top to come up with the solution—the right won't get it right, and the left won't have the competence to carry the day (nor could they in complex times). Put another way, it is very difficult to pull people up a ladder.

When "nothing works" over prolonged periods of time people eventually feel stuck, which is the situation we now have. When there is nowhere to turn people either give up or engage in rebellious actions that generate further frustration and/or acting out. When society exhausts positive options any notion of cohesion disintegrates, sense of self weakens or descends into small group self-protective cliques. Such a situation existed in the late 19th century as depicted by one of the founders of sociology Frenchman Emile Durkheim (1858–1917). He coined the term *anomie* defined as: "the state of normlessness, disorder, or confusion in a society when the standard norms and values are weak or unclear; this lack of social or ethical standards can lead to disconnection, deviance, and social instability among individuals." Anomie is a feature of the *system*: the structure not the individual. Anomie refers to a situation in which individuals are unable to achieve their goals or have unclear definitions of what those goals are. Durkheim said anomie represents a breakdown of social norms, values, or expectations within a society. It occurs when individuals feel disconnected or alienated from societal norms, resulting in feelings of aimlessness, disorientation, and moral confusion. Durkheim's most famous book is *Suicide* (1897) in which he documents that suicide rates increase with the spread of anomie.

In situations of pervasive anomie individual and small group alienation takes hold. Disruption, divisiveness, alienation, loneliness, and hopelessness dramatically increase. You can almost see and feel the breakdown of society getting worse week by week. Children and youth detect it as well.

Finally, there is some good news. Being stuck is better than living in a society where "nothing seems to work." When you are stuck you can start to work on ways of getting unstuck. If the bigger system is not very good at getting things done, it is likely not very good at preventing new initiatives within the system from taking hold. The silver lining is that positive initiatives at the bottom and middle have a better chance of taking hold and growing outward and upward. In fact, the new Six Secrets were made for this situation: Part 2 shows how and why, and Part 3 presents a whole new world. AI and the set of secrets in integrated action present a chance for humanity to regain the evolutionary potential for a remarkable future—something that is existentially unstable as I write these words.

· PART 1 ·
A Secret World

PART 2
Real Secrets Are Mysterious and Deep
THE NEW SIX SECRETS

· PART 3 ·
Systemness Change and the Future

Real Secrets Are Mysterious and Deep

Part 2 introduces the new *Six Secrets 2.0*. They are powerful and have depth. My intuition, given what I know about dynamic complexity and the world is that: if a secret is easily conveyed it is not much of a secret. Put another way, it is easy to implement a secret *superficially*. I get at them deeply by defining them with examples, including the leadership competencies that accompany them. Almost anyone can cultivate a good secret if they put time into understanding it, and above all help *others* understand and use it. The beauty of this is that when others use a good secret applied to their own setting they uncover *additional insights,* which increases the knowledge base for all. The secrets get deeper, shared, and continually refined.

The secrets are powerful guides to action all the more so when you consider the combination of the six; i.e., when you take into account their interaction effects that ramify. I always try to keep the number factors in play under 10—the mind can only handle so much. Of course, AI can handle much more as we will see in Part 3, but for now let's just say don't trust AI on its own.

My objective is to widely disseminate the knowledge of the secrets, encouraging its application in ways that promote positive outcomes and serve as a safeguard against undesirable forces. After all, the ideas come from good practice as of 2026. The magic I think is the untapped human ingenuity of those who have been left out of system change, especially those at the bottom (such as students and teachers). The encouraging news is that what we need *does come from practice*. The meta secret is keep refining practice as the source of secret specificity.

Over the past five years we have developed new ideas (based on innovative practice) with more precise and powerful language. Much of this new leadership talk contains new depictions of the secrets in action. In each of the six sets of secrets I will identify the "Leadership Quality" that marks the secret at work. These leadership qualities are newly formulated from our recent research and fit the secrets quite well. Then in Part 3 we will pull it all together in the service of *transforming the system*.

The New Six Secrets

I don't have a complete integrated new theory of the Six Secrets as a system solution. The situation is too much in flux. But I can promise that developing the new Six Secrets in action will put you on the right pathway. It will also set you up for Part 3 where we delve into the present and immediate future with strategies that launch the transformation in school systems. There is a latent readiness, especially among the young, to do something positive and big to change this world. If we can find the right strategies of starting, this movement and supporting it a lot can be accomplished in a short period of time. Starting slow with the right elements to go fast can create the possibilities of a "whole new world." The Six Secrets ingredients represent a "flywheel" that can establish vital momentum on a large scale in three or so years—before the end of this decade.

Consider this chapter as placing you squarely in the center of new system action. It is an invitation to expand your sphere of engagement. It is time to learn, think, and consider how your context could best relate to influencing and coping with the future. Further ideas on actual new plans is the focus of Part 3.

Here are the new Six Secrets with the associated "leadership competencies" attached.

1. Love your employees: Spirit work.

2. Connect peers with purpose: Contextual literacy.

3. Capacity literacy prevails: Connected autonomy.

4. Learning is the work: Legacy leaders.

5. Transparency rules: Trust and interact.

6. Systems learn: Systemness mindset.

1. Secret One: Love Your Employees: Spirit Work

Leaders command "spirit" when it is present every day in their actions and words. Spirit work represents the deep commitment of humans to preserving and enhancing all life in the universe—human and nature. It is the shared humanity and deep care and commitment for all living things and beings. It is not spiritual, in a religious sense; it represents a connection to, and appreciation of something larger than oneself. Spirit work in our use defines the development of self, well-being, and learning; it is the very purpose of education for all. We also define learning and leading as a universal goal, where everyone is simultaneously a learner and leader. Our "framework" is intended to define and guide the development of spirit work. It applies to children, youth, and adults. Spirit work can be defined as the actions and accomplishments that leaders and others undertake to enable everyone to cope, grow, and develop under the complex and adverse conditions of contemporary society. It can help people realize their purpose and place in today's world.

Spirit work has its roots in indigenous values and is embraced by increasing numbers of the young and the old across the globe. This connection and care for something beyond your immediate self is also missing in many individuals and societies, and as such undercuts being able to experience a sustainable life on this planet. Spirit work isn't just about living a healthy and good life. It's also about nurturing the planet we live on and caring for all its inhabitants. It's about an awakening to your presence, and your impact. Spirit work in education concerns well-being and learning, especially in their close relationship to each other. It applies to all participants. It needs to be a universal characteristic applying equally to all races, and the young and the old. Spirit work pertains to both individual practitioners and groups of varying scales (Fullan & Tinney, 2024).

I will start with highlighting what I said in 2008, then build on this with respect to the more complex and expansive meaning of "love those you lead, work and learn with in 2025." Theories can be very general or more grounded. We decidedly go for the latter. For our purposes—helping leaders thrive in complex times—theories need to be close to the action. Secret One takes us all the way back to the general theory of Douglas McGregor a half century ago. McGregor (1960) contrasted two theories of human motivation concerning behavior in the workplace, which he called Theory X and Theory Y.

Theory X Assumptions:

- The average human being has an inherent dislike of work and will avoid it if he or she can.

- Because of their dislike for work, most people must be controlled and threatened before they will work hard enough.

- The average human prefers to be directed, dislikes responsibility, is unambiguous, and desires security above everything else.

Theory Y Assumptions:

- If a job is satisfying, then the result will be commitment to the organization.

- The average person learns under proper conditions not only to accept but to seek responsibility.

- Imagination, creativity, and ingenuity can be used to solve work problems by a large number of employees.

We can go back even further (and encounter a negative version) from Frederick Taylor, a proponent of Theory X almost a century ago in his *Principles of Scientific Management* (1911/2007). According to Taylor's studies in the steel industry, work tasks could be broken down, and workers could be taught to perform them with maximum efficiency and productivity. Taylor (2007) developed four principles of scientific management:

1. Replace rule-of-thumb work methods with methods based on a scientific study of the tasks.

2. Scientifically select, train, and develop each worker rather than passively leaving them to train themselves.

3. Cooperate with the workers to ensure that the scientifically developed methods are followed.

4. Divide work nearly equally between managers and workers, so that the managers apply scientific management principles to planning the work, and workers actually perform the tasks (p. 31).

Taylor demonstrated, for example, how a worker could be taught to nearly quadruple the volume of pig iron he moved simply through optimal timing of lifting and resting. In roughly the same period (100 years ago) we saw a glimmer of the alternative to Taylor's heartless management remedy in the work of Mary Parker Follet. By 1925 as a Management Researcher and Consultant, Parker Folett had concluded that the more complex the change, the more crucial it is to involve those implementing it by "jointly determining" what should change and how to go about putting it into practice. Thus she said: "The goal of management is to foster unity not uniformity; to achieve greater integration via 'power with,' not 'power over;' the role of leaders is to 'produce other leaders'" (see Metcalf & Urwick, 2013). Unfortunately, her theories never caught on.

We can trace the theme of failing to involve implementers in the process of change all the way through this century moving through to 2008 (the original publication of Six Secrets) and on to 2025. Teachers and students have suffered from being mistreated and/or neglected as participants in a change process with few exceptions (the latter being the basis for our proposed solutions which leverage the new Secret One).

I find solid early evidence in a book with the cute title *Firms of Endearment* (Sisodia, Wolfe, & Sheth, 2007). The fact that it is grounded in evidence relative to named companies is especially helpful. Firms of endearment (FoEs), say Sisodia et al., endear themselves to stakeholders (customers, employees, investors, partners, and society). When these authors claim up front that *no stakeholder is more important than any other*, they are getting at the core of Secret One. FoEs create emotional value, experiential value, social value, and financial value. Customers, the authors say, "want to be in love, and if they don't find it, they'll settle for price and convenience" (p. 5).

I see no point in hashing through the last two and a half decades of research and practice of effective organizations in terms of how management treats employees and its impact on motivation and success. A good review is Julian Barling (2023): *Brave New Workplace: Designing Productive, Healthy, and Safe Organizations.* He marshals the evidence around "seven work characteristics": leadership, autonomy, belonging, fairness, growth, meaning, and safety. We will encounter these in a more integrated fashion across the secrets in this section (Part 2) and in Part 3 when I bring together the recommendations for "transforming systems." But let's take two more positive examples here: one from business, the other from education. Not surprisingly what effective school systems do looks very much like how good businesses function.

MIT Business professor, Zeynep Ton (2023) wrote a wonderfully grounded book called *The Case for Good Jobs: How Great Companies Bring Dignity, Pay & Meaning to Everyone's Work.* Studying an array of named companies, Ton shows "how market wages are not enough, and how turnover is ruinous" (p. 33ff).

Ton found that effective companies "hire the right people and train them well," "trust front-line employees to solve problems for customers," and "develop or retrain strong unit managers" (p. 70). Ton labels one set of examples as "managers are often unaware of how mediocre their system is" (p. 72). Simply speaking, ineffective organizations do not prioritize frontline workers, which is one of the keys to success.

The first triage, says Ton, is to:

- Raise pay

- Improve schedules

- Raise expectations

- Create clear career paths

- Give employees enough time to do their jobs (p. 182)

Notably Ton calls her book, *The Case for Good Jobs*. She supports her argument with evidence and company names. In our own empirical systems work on education we make the assertive case with solid evidence that good work and good learning is the essence of improving school systems. In *Whole Learners, Whole Systems* focusing on six school districts (actually five, as one is a county with several districts within it) we identified "good work" as consisting of four shared characteristics: shared vision, steady work, systemness, and symmetry (Fine, Rincón-Gallardo, & Fullan, in press).

In a second book focusing deeply on Anaheim Unified High School District (AUHSD is one of the six entities in the Fine et al. study) we go deeply into how AUHSD is transforming the culture of a high poverty, racially diverse district by altering just about everything for students, teachers, the community, and a variety of partners. It alters student voice and purpose, provides meaningful pathways and partnerships for graduates to be "good in society" and "for society," changes the nature of the roles of educators, and provides incentives and conditions for teachers and students to learn together. It celebrates, enables, and incentivizes every student and teacher to learn and be successful. Crucially, AUHSD employs specific mechanisms for students to develop from vague or no purpose to highly grounded purposes aligned with present and future possibilities. I describe this work later in this section deriving from AUHSD's partnership with Professor Mary Helen Immordino Yang (MHIY) in her breakthrough work on "Transcendent Thinking" (see MHIY, 2025).

"Transcendent Thinking" is a strategy that helps students develop from their present situation (the "here and now") where some 80% of students find little meaning or purpose. Through new guided learning experiences students are helped to realize a new purpose that helps them focus on the "then and thereafter." Within their present schooling they literally develop a new sense of purpose suited to present and future society (I take this up as a case study later in Part 2).

In short, the new strategic and empirical work that we are examining up close epitomizes the deep meaning of "love your employees." It is not theory. It is grounded transformation of learning and being.

A Long Way to Go

Perhaps the most accurate way of ending Secret One is to remind ourselves that each of six secrets has deep meaning: nuances if you like: "Subtle differences in meaning depending on tone or context." You don't win the day by just telling people how much you love them. With reference to our six secrets they are laced with inner meanings. The actions we are talking about are sophisticated, and heavily contextualized. Many school districts can look successful from a distance. But is the success built in?

Can the so-called successful district survive the turnover of a great leader? (Actually, our "six secret" organizations are more successful relative to turnover—see Secret Five about "Legacy Leadership.")

This is not to criticize the many excellent leaders and districts that are striving to make their districts successful, but rather to say that these days success is fragile. A good example is the research that we carried out in 2022. Mark Edwards and I ended up examining seven school districts from around the United States, northeast to southwest of varying sizes and other diverse characteristics. We published the book in 2022, Fullan and Edwards: *Spirit Work and the Science of Collaboration*. Choosing the title was interesting. We had earlier written about "moral purpose": raising the bar and closing gap with respect to literacy, numeracy, and high school graduation. All seven districts were doing well on these measures. As we gathered initial data Mark made the case to me that there was something more going on in these districts beyond moral purpose. It was deeper, more widespread, relentless, ubiquitous across whole districts from Jefferson County Public Schools (Kentucky) with some 100,000 students (150 schools) to Highline Washington School District, near Seattle, with 19,000 students (33 schools).

We chose the title: Spirit Work and the Science of Collaboration. We asked the seven superintendents individually and collectively what they thought of the title, "spirit work." We gave our definition—a brief version of what we presented at the beginning of this chapter. Without exception, pending a small or larger pause (spirit work was not a term much used in school district work) all seven said, "Yes" that is exactly what we are doing. The phrase Science of Collaboration is another story. I have since preferred the term "Connected Autonomy" because it recognizes equally the role of the individual and the group.

Mark then approached Margaret Wheatley, one of the founders of spirit work, and asked if she would do the honor of writing a preface (see her book: *Turning to One Another: Simple Conversations to Restore Hope to the Future*). In the preface Meg wrote: "[Spirit Work] shows what it looks like to be fully human, to experience the human spirit." And then:

> "Especially now—when life is under siege. When decisions are made that destroy human and planetary futures, when policies are designed to drive us apart, to push us into survival mode so we can be controlled by fear—now is the moment when we must step forward as champions for the human spirit. This is true spirit work, and we will accomplish this by turning to one another, consciously choosing to collaborate, and persevering amid increasing setbacks and pushbacks. This is not the work of cowards. It is the work of pioneers" (p. xiii).

It is a testament to the need for a second edition of *The Six Secrets* that very few of the seven districts have progressed since our study. Stated differently, conditions for success have dramatically worsened since 2023: Covid, greater loss of purpose and connection to schools, greater inequality, and overall weakening of school districts. To be successful these days requires greater capacity to understand what is below the surface.

Today, given greater complexity and immensely more entangled problems, it is crucial that our first secret be developed much more deeply. The true secret is: "live spirit work and ubiquitous collaboration time and again in many different ways through your actions." You have to embody all six secrets.

The hidden secret is the impact of the *combination* of all six as they *interact* over time. I call this simplexity: The smallest number of key factors that produce a measurable effect—factors that cover the waterfront so to speak, and that are amenable to being understood by practitioners (including very young ones). People become more loveable when you enact and live the other five secrets.

Keeping to the theme of this book we need new secrets welling up within the system that begin to establish new and different pathways to the future.

2. Secret Two: Connect Peers with Purpose: Contextual Literacy

As before I start with the "Leadership Dimension": "Contextual Literacy."

Contextual Literacy concerns one's knowledge of, commitment to, and caring for the situation in which one lives. For leaders (again, for young and old) this means that to lead effectively one has to "know," value, and commit to understand the context as a precondition for helping to support, enrich, and perhaps transform the context for all members. This concept contains several key elements that would be essential to become a lead learner. These key elements require some digging and presence. Joining a new organization or moving between classes or schools means becoming an apprentice, learning from those familiar with the setting or others also facing similar changes.

Leaders who are newcomers need to be both apprentices and experts—they bring some knowledge and skills to the new situation, and they have something new to learn. Their context has changed the moment they become leaders in their new reality. They immediately become part of the context upon arrival, influencing it through their actions or inaction. On top of this when the entire environment changes, when there is substantial system disruption (as was the case during the pandemic), everyone becomes an apprentice to a certain extent.

Contextual knowledge is essential for engaging effectively with those in the situation in order to develop the knowledge and commitment essential for system improvement. Contextual knowledge is immersion, trial and error, and growth through relationships and time. The relationships, to build on the spirt work, are not just with people, it is relationships with the environment including structures and processes. A leader becomes both agent and actor in the new realm. When you combine "spirit work" and "contextual literacy" you essentially create the conditions for compassionate, connected and committed leaders and members to improve and even transform "the setting in which they live" (Leadership Tool Kit (pp. 13–14)).

All through this century people in schools as we have seen have lost their sense of purpose—individually and collectively. To start fresh, we must revisit why we have schools. What is their purpose? Secondly, whatever the purposes they must become tangible for the people who live in the context. A serious problem that large systems face, one that becomes more perplexing in an ever more complex, diverse world, is how to achieve a degree of cohesion and focus in an otherwise fragmented environment. We might call this the too tight–too loose dilemma.

Focus the organization with sharp goals and tight accountability, and you get passive or alienated workers. Go for decentralized creativity, and you get drift and inertia. The key to achieving a simultaneously tight-loose organization lies more in *purposeful peer interaction* than in top-down direction from the hierarchy.

I thank my colleague Roger Martin and fellow researcher Sally Osberg for their detailed revelation of this secret. In their study of social entrepreneurship in developing countries where the roles of the experts and the roles of those living in the situation were vastly different, Martin and Osberg (2015) found that both groups were sources of expertise, knowledge, and insights. So-called expert knowledge is only one part of the solution. Effective leaders learn to draw on the wisdom of those not seen or classified as experts. External or new leaders are not afraid to display their knowledge about things they think they know, but they also are hungry to learn when it comes to areas about which they are less knowledgeable. More subtly they must realize in general that there may be things that 'they don't know what they don't know'.

It is not just a matter of commitment but also requires detailed knowledge about the culture and the variety of people and subcultures. Secrets one and two feed each other because spirit work and knowledge and commitment to build contextual literacy develop relational trust, increase focus, and build cumulative efficacy.

Secret Two is especially critical in *SSC 2.0* because the previous version (2008) failed to develop a sense of purpose on the part of the bottom and in many cases the middle. Put another way, in 2008, there was an implicit top-down assumption which tried "to use" peer interaction to cultivate a sense of purpose.

Such a strategy didn't work then, and certainly not now, where the agenda is more complex and contentious. Adding "contextual literacy" places the bottom and the middle in the center of action as proactive partners thereby enabling them to contribute to the development of our new systemness paradigm.

Success is not just a matter of commitment but also requires detailed knowledge about the culture and the variety of people and subcultures. Secrets one and two feed each other because spirit work and knowledge and commitment to build contextual literacy, develop relational trust, increase focus, and build cumulative efficacy.

It is easy to miss the nuances of Secret Two. Peer interaction must be purposeful and must be characterized by high-capacity knowledge and skills (Secret Three). More and more we want to reverse the line of influence: the bottom and middle influencing upward rather than receiving orders or manipulation from above. Moreover, the teaching and learning profession (students included) have not been set up for lateral learning within and across schools. For that we need more secrets.

3. Secret Three: Capacity Building Prevails: Connected Autonomy

"Connect peers with purpose," and "Connected Autonomy" obviously overlap. I have already shown that schools have lost their sense of purpose for the majority of students, and for many teachers. Whatever the action is relative to the first two secrets must be mediated by what kind of capacity building that is essential. Here I would say that the terrain is pretty rocky. It must play itself out in relation to what kind of capacity will be required. The heart of the latter is again another nuance which can be best appreciated by grappling with an essentially ambiguous concept: Connected Autonomy.

Connected autonomy is not a continuum. It is the single state of being simultaneously connected to, and autonomous within, a given context. We find the term collaboration too vague when it comes to sorting out what it means. Connected autonomy is also complex, but it allows one to explicitly consider connection to others, and commitment to one's own values and situation. It allows you to reflect on your degree of autonomy in each group situation, but also to recognize that autonomy is connected to a larger purpose, and intent. Connected autonomy enables you to consider your contributions to the group, what you are learning from the group, and how you are shaped by the group in support of your own agency. These contributions and learnings occur in a way that both you and the group are simultaneously benefitting. It is through the acts of engagement and reciprocity that connections can be deepened and enriched. It is also essential to consider the three concepts together in their two-way and multi-way interactions: spirit work, contextual literacy, and connected autonomy.

Capacity building concerns competencies, resources, and motivation. Individuals and groups are high in capacity if they possess and continue to develop knowledge and skills, if they attract and use resources (time, ideas, expertise, money) wisely, and if they are committed to putting in the energy to get important things done *collectively* and *continuously* (ever learning). As a secret capacity building has its share of nuances. In this case there are three myths that are simply wrong. One is that having high no-nonsense expectations for everyone is the best motivator. The second mistake is the false goal that you should seek the best *individual talent*. The third insight is to recognize that "too much autonomy," or "too much connection," can be problematic. You need a dynamic connection between the two as a natural state.

There are several tensions at play here. The first one assumes that "fear" is the most effective incentive (it can be if you have a gun to your head and the requested action does not require skill). Fear combined with high expectations is the opposite of our positive capacity builder that I identify below: high expectations combined with non-judgmentalism. Jack Welch (2001), CEO of General Electric for 20 years (1981–2001), become known as neutron Jack because he developed a policy of firing the lowest performing 10 or 20% of employees annually. Hectoring is not motivating in any walk of life. People do not function well (at least not for very long) when they are scared and angry.

A more subtle version of the first myth is Abrahm Lincoln's behavior as a leader that demonstrates the difference between judgment and judgmentalism. Lincoln did a good deal of concerted moral thinking about slavery. His position was unequivocal: "if slavery is not wrong, nothing is wrong." This opinion may not sound remarkable today, but it was certainly not the norm in Indiana and Illinois, where Lincoln grew up and worked, let alone in the South. His moral stance on slavery is not the point here; it's how he used it to approach the problem. He avoided judgmentalism. Lincoln conceived his task as engaging in "joint efforts to accomplish *society-wide* goals through the instrument of government" (Miller, 2002, p. 105; italics added).

Non-judgmentalism is a "secret of change" because it is so very heavily nuanced. You have to be able to hold a strong moral position without succumbing to moral superiority as your sole change strategy. As we sometimes put it "being right is not a strategy." Miller notes, "When we strive for some great good or oppose some great evil, it is extremely difficult not to spill out some of the goodness onto ourselves and the evil onto our opponents, creating a deep *personal* moral gulf. It is very difficult, in other words, when professing or striving for something righteous, to avoid self-righteousness and moral condemnation" (2002, p. 151; italics in original). Even more subtle perhaps is if your goal is to improve the behavior of a sensitive beginning teacher, one of the worse things you can do is to "roll your eyes" at the sight of an instance of bad teaching (there are many ways to roll your eyes without literally doing so).

The second adverse problem is overemphasizing individual talent. Pfeffer and Sutton (2000) note that it creates a focus on the individual rather than the collective. Evolutionary theory once more: when the environment turns nasty, people focus on self-preservation. Managers become more concerned with taking credit for their own good performance and blaming others for poor performance. One branch manager interviewed by Pfeffer and Sutton "focused only on his individual performance throughout our conversation, emphasizing the reasons he deserved more credit than he was getting. He never once described anything that he had done to help another branch manager, or described anything that another manager had done to help him" (pp. 126–127). Another subtly is found in Dan Pink's book, *Drive* (2009), when he quotes as recruiter who states that in a job interview if I sense "if you need me to motivate you, I probably don't want to hire you" (p. 32).

What about too much autonomy, or too much connection? With regard to the former, the person who doesn't want to work with anyone can be problematic but beware. Recall the teacher in the Marie-Claire vignette who was a loner. He was a good individual teacher, but the overall climate of the school was dysfunctional. So, understandably he kept to himself, until he experienced connection on a more productive basis. He and others who worked with him became successful as if he was a different person. Sometimes apparent mavericks can have a lot to offer in different circumstances. Change the context, and you sometimes change the person.

We can also see too much autonomy in the history of the teaching profession. Teachers and administrators have had negative experiences to the point that they have calcified. Teachers feel they are overmanaged and mistrusted. Managers come to feel that teachers are defensive and unreachable. Our solution is twofold. Do the hard work of breaking the cycle of mistrust (which admittedly will be hard to unseat, but that's the point—new leadership has to be that good). We can also set new welcoming conditions and expect new teacher leaders to take on this transformation to help develop better and more productive relationships. Second, don't take mistrust personally (it comes from a long tradition) while you work hard to change the hiring and leading norms to a positive "hire and cultivate talented people" which could have powerful impact on the future of teaching and learning.

Finally, you can have too much connection. Groupthink and Balkanization come to mind. Then there are the mixed breeds: One person's isolation is another person's solitude. The point is that people need to keep connection and autonomy in dynamic equilibrium.

In the meantime, we can review this "hire and culti-vate" strategy in terms of what I said in 2008, and what we are doing now in 2025 where in the case of AUHSD we have re-discovered the power of focusing on cultivating talent (see also Kirtman, 2025).

Hire and Cultivate Talented People: 2008

Toyota wins the prize for identifying and cultivating talent among all employees throughout the organization. Toyota's ongoing learning culture is amazing. But the company starts by attracting good people (because Toyota has a reputation for embodying the idea that "good people working with other good people get even better"). People want to work there in the first place: "The truth is that Toyota does like to start with good people who possess the *capacity* to become exceptional employees" (Liker & Meier, 2007, p. 18; italics in original).

Toyota pays the same careful attention to selecting and developing managers and coaches. The attributes it looks for in trainers consist of willingness and ability to learn, adaptability and flexibility, genuine caring and concern for others, patience, persistence, willingness to take responsibility, confidence and leadership, and a questioning nature. In the direct skill domain, Toyota stresses observation and analytical ability, communica-tion skills, attention to detail, job knowledge, and respect of fel-low employees (Liker & Meier, 2007, p. 72).

In some ways, organizations that are on top of Secret Three turn the tables and constantly ask themselves (humbly and then confidently), "Why would great people want to work here?" And if they get that answer right, their employees become their best recruiters. The most successful companies (as I define them through the six secrets) have decided that human resources is too important to leave to one unit. They have repositioned and refashioned human resources as a central, integrated prime driver of the corporate culture. This is true of all the firms of endearment. (Sisodia et al., 2007, wrote a whole chapter on "the decline and fall of human resources.")

I must say humbly that my argument in 2008 was not taken up much in the ensuing years. In retrospect the main reason was that I failed to realize that the system itself was not conducive to leveraging the secrets. More than this as you will recall 2008 was the beginning of what I called the "while we were sleeping decade" only to have a rude awakening to what I now call the deeply "stuck" period.

Twenty years later we have a second chance. The problem of poor leadership is more pronounced now, and the need for a different kind of leadership is palpable. We need to check out the new impetus for altering HR to become more proactive in helping to transform the culture of education. If we start changing the hiring practices, and the support therein, we begin to alter the future direction.

Hire and Cultivate Talented People: 2025

Just as AUHSD was focusing deeply and persistently on transforming its culture Lyle Kirtman (2025) published his new book: *Shaping the Future*. The second of his four Leadership Pivots is: "Moving from Human Resources to Talent Management: Solving the Workforce Crisis." (We include the other three pivots in Part 3 as they fit with and confirm our overall solution: Find your North Star; Set High Expectations for staff and students; Employ Intrinsic Accountability with Student and Staff agency.)

Kirtman lays out a procedure whereby:

- Talent management allows staff members to utilize their strengths and their values to ensure an effective work-life balance.

- Talent management requires a collaborative effort among all entities to develop the workforce to meet current and future needs for students.

- Talent management allows a pathway for staff to advance in their career.

- Talent management allows organizations to make systematic decisions about the development of staff.

"Talent management allows organizations to focus on excellence" (Kirtman, 2025, p. 81).

In the short time we have been using Talent Development in AUHSD we have noticed that instead of not thinking at all about HR, or assuming that it has nothing to do with them, staff are now more conscious about building current and future peers. More than that Talent Development is turning out to be a very "sticky phrase" in 2025. It fits well with our new systemness phenomenon. When there is such great vulnerability to the job market and the nature of work with AI and other forces people are more ready to identify with their job market and the need for a more stable future. They are more prepared potentially to act jointly with good leaders to help develop a better society. In our new language they are ready for greater "proximity to practice" in order to enhance the future (see our new "Learning Flywheel" that consists of: Proximity, Specificity, Speed/Momentum, Part 3).

Secret Three obviously feeds into Secret Four, perhaps the most central to the future effectiveness of the organization.

4. Secret Four: Learning Is the Work: Legacy Leaders

Secret Four is the longest and deepest secret. This is so because Secret Four is where the other five secrets play themselves out. This is why we frequently remind people that what counts most is what happens in between training sessions and meetings. It is as Elmore told us a deep secret, hard to learn, and requires continual honing. Legacy leaders—those who want to have a present and lasting impact—are simultaneously engaged in several dimensions of leadership. They are aware of being effective leaders in the immediate situation (through spirit work, contextual literacy, and connected autonomy); they "model" what such leadership looks like; they act as mentors, guides, and navigators and nurture a culture of leaders learning from each other. The end result is that the main mark of effective leaders is not only their impact on the bottom line of increased well-being and learning, but also how many good leaders they leave behind— this is "legacy leader."

We need to get some terms straight before delving further into Secret Four. Frederick Taylor sought *prescription*. Today we need to figure out and pursue *precision*. Taylor wanted to achieve 100% efficiency, whereas we need to strike a dynamic balance between *consistency* and *innovation*. Jobs vary in their degree of routine versus nonroutine work, but we will see in this chapter that the consistency-innovation continuum applies to all jobs, whether they involve doctors and nurses washing their hands, automobile manufacturing, the use of intravenous catheters, improving literacy, or reducing the number of high school dropouts.

The essence of Secret Four concerns how organizations address their core goals and tasks with relentless consistency, while at the same time learning continuously how to get better and better at what they are doing. In this chapter we will consider how to reconcile the consistency-innovation dilemma in a variety of settings. I will be precise by using concrete examples. And then we will see how organizations go about ensuring that consistency and innovation get built into the culture of everyday work.

The secret behind "learning is the work" lies in our integration of the precision needed for consistent performance (using what we already know) with the new learning required for continuous improvement (recent innovations that teach us more). The problem is that the current situation requires *new work!* The details, specificity in action, need to be developed with and by those doing the work (learning)—students and teachers among others.

This new mode takes us to what we now call "specificity without imposition." What is the best approach to operationalize complex ideas in ways that enable early access and comprehension. Richard Elmore nailed this problem in 2004. He noted that "improvement is more a function of learning to do the right thing in the setting in which you work" (p. 73). He elaborates: "The problem [is that] there is almost no opportunity for teachers to engage in continuous and substantial learning about their practice in the setting in which they actually work, observing and being observed by their colleagues in their own classrooms and classrooms of other teachers in other schools confronting similar problems of practice" (p. 127). There was/is no opportunity because people will not share when there is the risk of being judged (often unfairly). By 2025, the context has changed enormously. We have a whole new ballgame where the work is more complex, with high reward being possible but more risky. Solutions are more sophisticated, and harder to develop. In the new culture teachers learn together to do what works to accomplish complex learning (such as "transcendent thinking" for example—see section on TT, p. 80). They come to be able to demonstrate and describe what it looks like in practice.

It has always been the case that students and teachers must "learn in context or learn superficially." There are subtleties here (as always in complex work). Lyle Kirtman and I have always said that "sometimes you have to go outside to get better inside" (Kirtman & Fullan, 2016, p. 15). In some ways there is not enough learning going on in context that is worth learning. As we improve present contexts—the true value of collaboration— there will be more to learn within and across schools.

People are unsure about what to do and discouraged by the combination of stress and unclear pathways. Well-being *and* Learning figure prominently and differently in the present than they did 20 years ago with the weird new proposition that we may know more about well-being than learning. This doesn't mean that well-being needs less attention, but it does mean that new learning needs to be at the core of development.

It is no surprise that ill-being has skyrocketed over the past decade for both educators and students. In my books the superstar researcher on Social and Emotional Learning is Professor Kimberly Schonert-Reichl (KSR), first at University of British Columbia, now at University of Illinois at Chicago. KSR and her colleagues have done a huge amount of interrelated studies. Fortunately for us they completed a massive review and summary of their findings (Schonert-Reichl et al., 2023). They found a major increase in the number of studies on the relationship between teacher and student well-being. In summary, they say:

> "The research underscores the critical importance of nurturing both educator and student well-being to create engaging and productive learning environments where both teachers and students can thrive" (pp. 11–12).

But this is the beginning not the end of the argument. The key question for our purposes ("learning is the work") is how to improve *learning*: what are the "up close strategies" (proximity to learning, and specificity of practice) that portray well-being and learning *co-developing*. The answer is that there are hardly any examples that integrate well-being and learning that show impact on deep learning such as on global competencies (there are a few that I will highlight later, but my point is that they are rare). Ironically, strategies for well-being are necessary to combat *bad education systems* (see Joanna Rizzotto's (2025) doctoral dissertation on "restorative practices" as an antidote to bad education systems): "Shifting the schema of schooling: The introduction of generative regulation theory." Joanna shows how crucial restorative practices are but did not link this to deeper learning.

The key question for me is how is "new learning faring" these days. My conclusion is that well-being is a necessary but insufficient strategy for altering the "learning system" that we need now and in the future. We seem to be aware of the terrible ill-being conditions, and some of the marginal improvement strategies, but are mostly oblivious to the deeper learning strategies that might be required to save a world heading for destruction. I will present a few unusual examples that I consider curious, followed by new cases that directly address the need for learning as integral work for coping and being successful in a complex dysfunctional world.

How is this for a curious example. Jhonel Morvan was born in Haiti. He emigrated to Ontario Canada as a 23-year-old. He worked his way up the education system, worked in the ministry of education, and is currently an assistant superintendent in one of the 72 school districts in Ontario. Jhonel completed his doctorate in 2023. His dissertation was titled: *A Quest for Equity in School Mathematics in Ontario: Connecting Black Secondary School Experiences and Achievement to Principal Leadership.* PhD Dissertation, Brock University, Ontario, Canada. The students were from the Toronto District Schools Board. TDSB which has about 246,000 students, with 12% or just under 30,000 Black students.

In his dissertation he took the total population of Black students at grade 9 and measured two things: The Math achievement of students on the grade 9 mathematics test administered by the provincial assessment agency and the "Emotional

Well-being Scores" that TDSB administers to all students periodically. The EWB is based on the following six questions:

1. Over the last school year, how often have you felt:
   Good about yourself

2. Over the last school year, how often have you felt:
   Hopeful about the future

3. Over the last school year, how often have you felt:
   You liked the way you look

4. Over the last school year, how often have you
   felt: Lonely

5. Over the last school year, how often have you felt:
   Nervous or worried

6. Over the last school year, how often have
   you felt: Sad

Morvan found that Black students had the *highest* EWB scores of any subgroup in TDSB (which is a highly diverse district), and among the *lowest results* in grade 9 math scores. High well-being and low academic achievement! What is going on here? Morvan and I have been delving into what might have been the explanation. I leave the reader to speculate. Perhaps some secondary school principals are tending to the well-being needs of Black students, and/or the Black community and peer groups have certain social support systems. We have no firm explanations yet. At this stage we treat it as a curious case. But we do know that their apparent well-being had little to do with learning at school. The fact that they did poorly in math shows that "teaching and learning" was weak.

A second example comes from Russell Bishop, a Maori Professor from New Zealand who was funded for over 10 years by the NZ government to foster closer relationships and better learning among Maori students and families on the one hand, and teachers and schools on the other hand. The purpose was to develop better relationships *and* improved learning (Bishop, 2023). NZ has a 17% Maori population (just under 1 million people). I asked Russel to send me one of his graphs that I found most interesting. I reproduce it here.

Figure 4.1 is remarkably revealing with respect to some of the subtleties of system change. Bishop made the crucial distinction between foster better *relationships* between teachers and students and their families, and better *learning*. He made the crucial

Figure 4.1: The Relations-Based Learner Profile (Bishop, 2023)

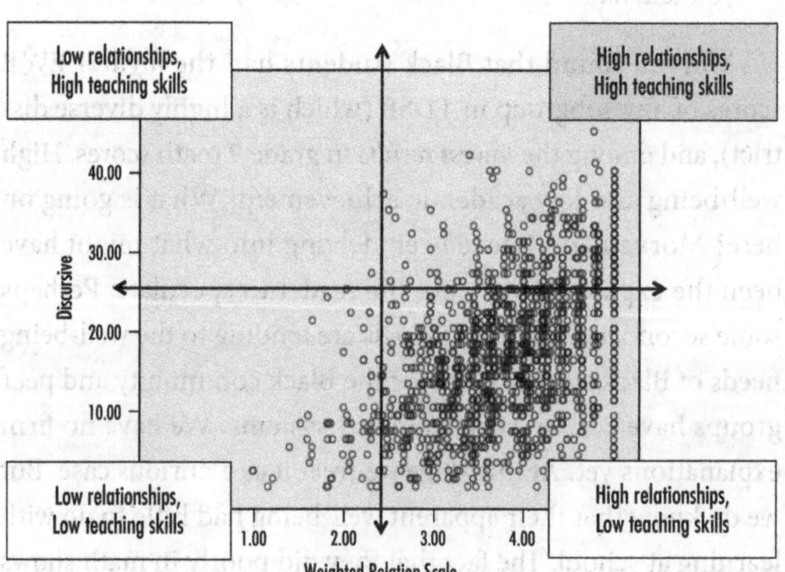

discovery that it is possible to improve one (relationships), without improving the other (learning). This finding is crucial, and in many ways quite revealing. It seems easier to think "let's improve relations," and then unwittingly to fail to appreciate that changing learning/pedagogy is a separate but connected dimension. Changing both in tandem and deeply is the winning combination.

In Bishop's case the short explanation is that teachers and communities did an effective job of building positive relationships with "student and their families" on the one hand, and the "school" (bottom right quadrant) on the other hand. But they made limited progress on "teaching skills" I make no more than the inference here that building relationships per se is not necessarily related to *effective learning*.

In short, there is much more to learning than relationships and teaching strategies as we will see in a moment with "Transcendent Thinking," and the linking of cognition along with relationships as we will see shortly in the Mary Helen Immordino-Yang (2025) and Zaretta Hammond examples.

In the rest of this chapter I will open up the question of what is "powerful learning." This potentially powerful twin of well-being has gone missing. When it comes to the secret of "learning is the work" twinning well-being and new learning is the future. In a complex, dysfunctional world the absence of good combinations of well-being and new learning negatively affects *all students*. It turns out that integrating well-being and learning is complex (why wouldn't it be) but is graspable by the average 10-year-old (actually 2-year-old), and the average teacher. This is so because this new work causes the development of individual and collective capacity and commitment of those learning. I might say that it comes natural to humans (when enabled) and unleashes the desire to tackle the most complex problems. Why? Because it becomes *personal*—to both the individual and the group. In short, we need more powerful examples of *learning*. Secret Four in effect reveals that the traditional structure and culture of schooling is fundamentally inimical to the kind of learning we need in order to cope and thrive in the world that has evolved to the present. Unlike some others, I don't think we should abandon schools, but rather we should transform them to places of social learning that includes the possibility that new learning could help change society. Further I believe that many students and teachers want to or could come to want to help lead the transformation that would be required. This is the essence of the new Six Secrets, and corresponding actions in Part 3 that could help carve the pathway to a new future. Let's get started.

Transcendent Thinking

Transcendent Thinking (TT) consists of going beyond the "here and now," to the "what if and then." It's opposite is learning that is confined to the immediate situation that is, "Context dependent"—being constrained by what is. There is a new radical solution in the air and it comes from the work of neuroscientist Professor Mary Helen Immordino-Yang and her CANDLE group (Center for Affective Neuroscience, Development, Learning and Education) at USC, Rossier in Southern California. Our team is now part of a multi-party group that consists of CANDLE, Anaheim, and our team that includes Neuroscientist and Child Psychiatrist, Jean Clinton.

TT meets our transforming criteria: it's radical, proximate to practice, and immersed in specificity. To clear up any confusion, "contextual literacy" is valuable, largely because it provides insights into how to improve the existing context. We seek valuable contextual literacy because we (and the school communities in question) want to alter the community for the better. To put it bluntly, if the context is not supporting new learning, we want to change it so that it does. Thus, we are developing TT through new practices that change the structure and culture of existing schools because currently they patently do not work to engage students in new learning.

Most of us are familiar with the phrase "the grammar of schooling"—the deeply ingrained structure and culture of traditional schooling (Tyack & Cuban, 1997). After decades of banging our heads against the wall our group is shifting to making and testing the changes in goals, structure, and culture that we think are essential and on the right track. We are now able to test these ideas in real time in close partnership with students, teachers, schools, districts, and communities. It involves working with students and educators to co-develop breakthroughs in learning. The new work on cognitive development is essential to this transformation.

It is not just genes that determine who we become. The brain develops in a use-dependent way; experiences build the brain. Behaviors that get repeated over and over wire up and form networks of connections. Relationships are an active ingredient in this brain development. In terms of age-related brain growth, we now know that by age five or so children's brains, on the average, reach some 90% of the size of the adult brain. Growth in brain connectivity—a second spurt if you will—occurs during adolescence (ages 10–25, or so). Much of ordinary schooling, based on fact acquisition with little connection to relevant lived experience renders only temporary memory and little "stickiness" or retention. In other words, it bores kids to death.

In addition, we have known for some time that exposure to violence and trauma also changes the brain in significant ways including hypervigilance and accelerated "thinning" of key brain regions of the cortex.

The new TT work is a radical doable intervention that dramatically can change the learning and well-being of adolescents. Immordino-Yang and others first in the lab, and now in all of Anaheim Union High School District (AUHSD) with its 26 schools and 20,000, students, new "Transcendent Learning" is occurring that has profound life-changing impact on students, both in the present and long term. Preliminary findings compare evidence from laboratory experiments using magnetic resonance imaging (MRI), with deliberate school district practices intended to develop greater "transcendent thinking" and corresponding behavior in teenagers, i.e., thinking that occurs within and beyond the "here and now."

Immordino-Yang started with a sample of 65 teens:

"We shared short documentary-style stories with participants, first in a private interview, and then again when while they lay in the fMRI scanner. By comparing individuals' psychological responses when discussing their feelings with the neural activity patterns they showed in the scanner, we began linking people's responses and ways of thinking about the world to underlying neurobiological mechanisms" (Immordino-Yang, 2025).

Here is what Immordino-Yang and her colleagues found:

"By listening closely to teenagers' reflections and observing their brain activations as they lay in the scanner [we] discovered that thinking that ranges flexibly from the here and now. . .to the past, the future and everything else, seems to literally build their brains. During such wide-ranging, emotionally powerful, reflective thinking—which we call transcendent because it soars beyond the moment—key brain networks activated and deactivated in complex, dynamic patterns which our data indicated grew and strengthened their connections" (Immordino-Yang, 2025).

Over the past decade, Immordino-Yang and her team proceeded to interview students, presenting them stories, getting their reactions, and capturing the cross talks among their brain networks. Putting various measures together, the researchers found that adolescents who were motivated to talk about the bigger picture, who sought "to figure out the deeper meaning of what they had learned" (transcendent thinking) showed evidence of differing brain growth with coordination between differing areas of the brain, than those whose comments were limited to the "here and now."

Their conclusion is that thinning (pruning) of the prefrontal cortex during the early teenage years (as unused parts of the brain are pruned) was less evidenced for "about half of the teens in the sample. Transcendent thinking predicted increases in cortical volume." Such experience apparently caused their brain to grow (greater thickness of the prefrontal cortex) "even more than normal pruning shrank it."

The researchers also probed wider issues. "We asked [our teenagers] to report on any violent acts they had witnessed or heard in their community and then interviewed them about their understanding of the causes of and possible solutions to such social problems. We found that teens who reflected more on the broader historical cultural, or social context of the crimes they had witnessed, rather than simply blaming the implicated individuals' bad behavior in that moment. In sum, the more transcendent thinking students engaged in, the less thinning we found in the [pre-frontal cortex]."

There is much more to the CANDLE groups work with respect to deep transformative learning (listen to Immordino-Yangs in-depth podcast (2025)). Meanwhile, we are collaborating with AUHSD and others in practice. The TT initiative has extended to a formal agreement in 2024 to partner with AUHSD students. The development of "Transcendent Thinking" as a formal program has now extended to all students in the district. Accordingly, the redesign of the whole system is underway (Berry, Matsuda, & Fullan: *The Future of Public Education*, in press). TT is being integrated in key elements of the AUHSD learning activities: the commitment to purpose and belonging, the Capstone and 5Cs portfolio, pursuit of competencies, Teacher Performance Assessment, Performance Portfolios, Soap Box presentations, and more. TT activities are ubiquitous, comprehensive, and used to assess students' progress. Above all they are visible for all to see.

The amount of scrutiny, knowledge, and sheer attraction to this work is bound to increase. Already there are two doctoral dissertations near completion:

- Emily Gonzalez (forthcoming), a Rossier doctoral student of Dr Immordino-Yang is focusing on the details of Performance Task Assessments (PTAs) to get at the specificity of TT content. The tentative title of her dissertation is: "Human Development at the Heart: A Multi-Case Study of Innovative Teaching in a Public Secondary School District."

- Natalie Fensterstock (forthcoming) UCLA doctoral student is similarly near the end of her data gathering for her dissertation. Tentative Title: Graduating students who are good *for* society and Good *in* Society. (I am a member of her dissertation committee.)

Because this new work is so different, so engaging, so powerful, and so natural to the daily work, it promises to be endorsed widely. Learning is the work is a secret that people will want to get to know and keep.

There is an interesting paradox about complex secrets. The more complex they are, the harder they are to steal. I think this is why "great companies" (Ton, 2023) and great school districts like AUHSD are such great sharers. They want to contribute to the wider good. They are not worried about their competition taking their best ideas. You can't steal depth! Moreover, they want others to shine because it will be good for all, and AUHSD in turn will learn from them. Another example of new in-depth new work follows.

Emotion and Cognition Meets Learning: Zaretta Hammond (2026)

Zaretta Hammond is a Teacher Educator and Researcher whose work for the past 30 years has focused on how to activate the deep learning work of students whose learning interests fail to be cultivated by regular schooling. She especially focuses on Black students. Fundamentally she is also concerned about all students who are disconnected to deeper learning. If the reader has gathered one main message of my book, it is that good learning has turned out to be problematic for the majority of all students. Good learning—using what we know about emotion, cognition, social development to survive and thrive in a deeply complex world—turns out to be complex to say the least. But because it is achievable under the right conditions, and as such becomes deeply motivational for individuals and collectivity's, it can also become an active attraction for even large school systems in a fairly short time (about 3–5 years). For example, this is becoming the case in AUHSD where transcendent thinking is rapidly gaining favor.

Taking a combination of things we already know Zaretta is setting out "to reimagine schooling and create something more equitable for all students" (p. 3). Yes, the systemic obstacles are massive and deeply rooted, but sometimes we have enough clarity about the nature of the solutions that it becomes an option "worth fighting for." Zaretta states that the path forward is twofold—altering the traditional roles of teachers and students: "First, we need to re-orient ourselves around the student as primary actor in teaching and learning. . .[noting that we have overused the term. . .*student centered*], while we develop 'the cognitive capital' or 'learning power' of students. Second, we need to level up our professional learning processes and structures. . . We will have to learn how to help teachers to coach students to change their learning moves" (p. 5).

Note, this is essentially what "Transcendent Thinking" does!

The solution (instructional equity, science of learning, and cognitive understanding) forms the basis of the new learning. Zaretta notes the "cognitive redlining" (unwitting or deliberate) attributing low capability to certain students—for race and/or socio-economic status reasons can limit what is expected and given to a student to learn. It is not enough to offer innovative student-centered learning options without the development of information processing skills. Zaretta states: "they can be implemented in ways that are shallow, performative, and are still grounded in the pedagogy of compliance" (p. 25).

Low expectations and/or poor pedagogy can leave teachers focusing on "information as learning" (i.e., memorization), while deeper learning focusses on "thinking" ("structuring information for processing that leads to meaning making" (Hammond, p. 35)). Drawing on Vygotsky's *Zone of Proximal Development,* Zaretta notes that "cognitively independent students routinely stretch past their growing learning edge" (p. 38).

Zaretta notes six higher level learning competencies: "master of rigorous content, critical thinking, ability to work collaboratively, effective oral or written communication, learning how to learn, developing and maintaining an academic mindset" (p. 39). Note that in our deep learning we have six competencies that overlap with the six just stated, and four learning competencies that correspond to Zaretta's socio-emotional, and cognitive learning skills (Fullan & Quinn, 2024). In referring to 21st-century skills and our six global competencies, Zaretta observes: "Both sets of skills are essential for all students to reach their full potential" (Hammond, 2026, p. 40). Information processing skills are essential for 21st-century students:

> "Information processing prowess expands exponentially as students get more competent at processing new content that deepens their understanding. As students' competence grows, so does their confidence. As they experience more confidence, they are more inclined to stretch themselves cognitively and let go of dependent learning behaviors to reach higher levels of mastery in a subject area or with a skill" (pp. 42–43).

There are much more detail and elements, but the consistent themes for students and teachers alike is "Shifting from a pedagogy of compliancy toward a pedagogy of possibility" (p. 65). There are also a lot more what I call situation-based "Change Management" ideas that must be employed linked to the situation in question (see our discussion in Part 3). Such change is a complex learning proposition for all parties. Zaretta names four "mindsets" from Farrington et al.'s (2012) review of *Teaching Adolescents to Become Learners:*

1. I belong to this academic community.

2. My ability and competence grow with my effort.

3. I can succeed at this.

4. This work has value for me (pp. 117–119).

There are many more ideas in Zaretta's book and I recommend it as a guide to full action. It ties together the ingredients of system change: Belonging, Purpose, Emotion, Cognitive Development, Social Cohesion—these concepts linkable but only when you do so explicitly.

We need many more examples of the breakthrough work that MHIY and Zaretta Hammond represent—putting these ideas into practice and assessing their efficacy in improving emotional and cognitive connections in the service of deep learning.

At this point I am sure readers are saying to themselves: Sounds complicated. Is it doable? Is it worth it?

Well, it is complex, and also doable. This secret is "learning is the work." Judging what we have seen in this chapter when teachers have a chance to experience this new work, and when they are supported in these efforts, they readily take to it—lots of them accelerated by peer contagion and student engagement. Any qualified teacher will take to the new concepts when supported, and when there is a plan to engage the whole system change. At first many teachers are doubtful or resistant to change. Their experience tells them that this too shall pass: "The more things change the more they stay the same." But when it contains the different and uplifting elements we have seen in "Transcendent Thinking" and "Rebuilding Students" Learning Power sparks fly. First a few change, then some more, then the word gets around. Some teachers (and we have heard this explicitly in AUHSD) say, "Wow! This is why I came into teaching! To make a difference at the individual and school system level in the current and future lives of students, and perhaps even in our corner of society." This new "societal enhancing tide" can become visible within two years and then accelerate once the new flywheel is going. It is flat-out doable.

It is worth it? Compare it to any teacher's day in 2025. Compare it to groups of people in a community of one or more schools. Compare it to where you think society is trending. It is no contest when you compare the excitement of TT to the boring lives of most students and teachers currently in school. Still, radical new change is very difficult to get started.

Where to Next

When we knew what the agenda was: literacy, numeracy, and high school graduation, we knew what to prepare for. Now we don't. And there is chaos anyway as to what awaits us as we finish one level of schooling or another. The good school systems we work with are now learning on the job (i.e., in schools) what is needed today and tomorrow in real time.

Of all the secrets "learning is the work" is the most transformed in this 2.0 publication. I lay the groundwork here and delve into specific new usages in Part 3. The big lesson is that essential learning for coping and thriving now (2026) is less and less *prior* to being on the job, and more and more *During the work itself!*

Given the ambiguity, tensions, uncertainties, and challenges in contemporary society, along with developments in artificial intelligence, there is a need to reconsider how change, stress, and opportunity are managed moving forward. In Part 3 you will encounter the proposed solutions. Included in this will be exciting, practical, new, and deeper strategies for developing, managing, and leveraging innovations in 2026 and beyond. These powerful insights led by those closer to practice (students, teachers, all those engaged in action, and "yes" machines, etc.) will be deep and immediate. They include ideas related to innovation, proximity to practice, specificity, speed, triangulation of educators, students, and yes, "machines." We will also find greater "quadrangulation" (sorry) with business and work communities as a fourth partner.

A crucial commonality across the secrets is *specificity and interaction* (see Figure 4.2). What is especially powerful in the new Six Secrets is that they all have a degree of "specificity and groundedness." The problem of change is not so much that some of the best ideas are resisted but rather that people don't understand them at a degree of specificity or what they might actually mean in practice. Our best proposals have "precision without prescription." Working through the details of potentially good ideas is best served through use and support by peers who have used the ideas. Along with specificity is the crucial role of "interaction." Collaboration or our better concept of connected

Figure 4.2: The Field of Interaction for Local Transformation

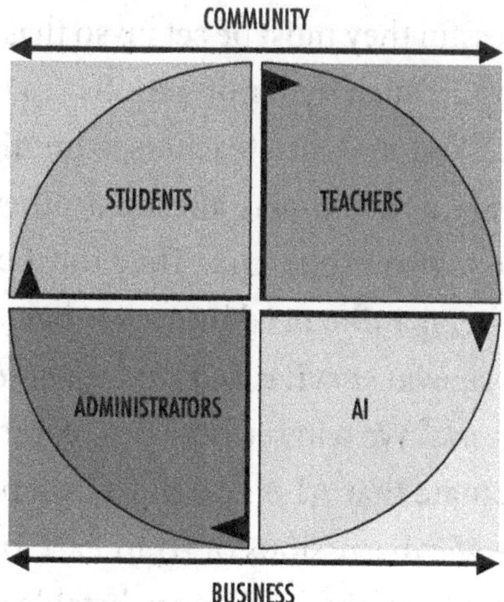

autonomy is essential for working through good, powerful ideas. The Six Secrets as a set bring the collective message that teaching is notoriously "the lonely profession" with not nearly enough collective interaction and continuous development. Incidentally any notion that AI could replace teachers suffers from "misplaced concreteness." Highly successful districts that we work with (such as Ottawa Catholic and Anaheim high school district) integrate AI including enabling teachers and students to work more deeply together. Purposeful, specific interaction and continuous development is the key.

In the original version of SSC, we saw what "learning is the work" was like in 2008. Dynamic companies like Toyota had an impressive discipline of innovation and learning with cross-cutting mechanisms of generating up-close development and continuous refinements. Let me say now that 2026 and following is and will be nothing like that. Ambiguity and unpredictability are working at non-linear warp speed. This means that "learning is the work" is urgent every day. The school districts we work with are engaged in such ambiguity and dynamic action all the time. To be successful they must be set up so that their structures and cultures support such dynamic actions. To use a new word, they are "agentic." Yes, students, teachers, administrators, and AI proactively interact, and *mutually* affect one other. Communities and businesses are also in the mix. They must become good at influencing and being influenced by each other.

In short, those who survive and thrive will be exemplars of "learning is the work." We will see how this works is Part 3.

Let me punctuate that AI is and must be a partner (see also the long and specific discussions of AI in Part 3). We now know that AI can be an interactive and unpredictable partner. It is not conscious, but for all our purposes (secrets of change), it might as well be. There is great danger in AI, but also great upside. Furthermore, its presence is ubiquitous and inevitable. It will insert itself whether we like it or not. Our challenge now is to figure out "how to like and leverage AI" for humanity!

Ethan Mollick's (2024) advice in *Co-Intelligence* is as good a way to start any:

"As artificial intelligence proliferates, users who intimately understand the nuances, limitations, and AI tools are uniquely positioned to unlock AI's full potential" (p. 48).

His four guidelines are intriguing and invitational:

Principle 1: Always Invite AI to the Table.

Principle 2: Be the Human in the Loop.

Principles 3: Treat AI Like a Person (But Tell It What Kind of Person It Is).

Principle 4: Assume that This Is the Worst AI You Will Ever See.

The leadership competency cluster for this secret is "legacy leadership." The mark of your own legacy is not just the impact on the bottom line of student learning, but also how many leaders (teachers and students alike) you have left behind who carry on perhaps even better than you did. It is going to take two or three generations to turn the negative tide of what has happened so far in the 21st century. When it comes time to retire, why not depart as a momentum maker of a new and better era!

It's time for the final two secrets to round out the complete picture: Transparency Rules and Systems Learn.

5. Secret Five: Transparency Rules: Trust and Interact

Leadership Skill: Trust and Interact

From 1984–1987, Ronald Reagan famously said on several occasions about the Soviet Union: "trust, but verify." He didn't trust the Soviet Union, but he needed a deal about the arms race and the cold war. These days there is much more not to trust, and it comes from many sources and angles. One could say you don't know who to trust. What are the leadership skills here? It is a strange combination, support those who are close to you, but don't rule out the mavericks. Sometimes you need "impressive empathy". . .attempting to understand those who seem against you. Also known as "perspective-taking" the ability to understand the thoughts, feelings, and experiences of others. Other times those who seem to support you often end up with a very different agenda. Sorting this our requires that "transparency rules" because within dynamic complexity in a world society gone rogue mystery is a mile deep. To a certain extent new choices will emerge or can be unearthed. Be a postmodern anthropologist. You never know what you will unearth.

Transparency rules because it is open to surprise—whatever it finds so to speak. This secret brings judgment to the fore, digging to uncover the nuances of a dynamic world that has the potential to create or destroy. Biologist and Pulitzer Prize winner E.O. Wilson put it this way:

> "Science owns the warrant to explore everything deemed factual and possible, but the humanities borne aloft of both fact and fantasy, have the power of everything not only possible, but conceivable" (Wilson, 2007, p. 70).

Transparency has the license to look and help sort out (along with the other secrets) what is desirable in a given era—say the next decade.

When I hear a leader talk about new possibilities or models, I first look for the specificity. If it stays at the general level, chances are that the leader does not have a grasp of the model in action. In that case, "the emperor has no clothes," but might look good from a distance. Let's call it the imposter syndrome. Instead, as I have argued we need to know the degree of "proximity to practice" and its corresponding "specificity." We can then delve deeper and assess its potential.

More than this we must test our own models by putting them out for scrutiny. More still, because we are at a deep inflection point, not knowing what should be next, transparency can serve as a search for new ideas. In this sense Secret Five represents an innovation zone. We need Secret Five in order to innovate and test new ideas models seeking other possibilities to what we are now doing. Transparency rules because in times of complex transition nobody knows what is coming next, and thus to a certain extent we should have an exploratory mindset, coupled with a testing orientation to those ideas that they see as potentially fruitful. Transparency is both experimental and developmental. This is where we are in 2026.

We see the simple power of what I call "mere transparency" in the economist Paul Collier's fascinating and disturbing account (2007) of the state of the world's poorest countries, *The Bottom Billion*. The hero, as Collier calls him, is Emmanuel Tumusiime-Mutebile, then governor of the Central Bank of Uganda and formerly the permanent secretary of the Ministry of Finance and Planning. As Collier tells the story, when the Ministry of Finance devised a survey to track public expenditure, it came up with the depressing result that only 20% of the money that the government released for primary schools, other than for teachers' salaries, actually reached the schools. What to do?

One way would have been to tighten the top-down system of audit and scrutiny, but they had already tried that and it patently doesn't work. So Tumusiime-Mutebile decided to try a completely different approach: scrutiny from the bottom-up. Whenever the Ministry of Finance disbursed funds, it notified the local media and sent posters to schools detailing their allocations. He repeated the tracking survey three years later. Now, instead of 20% getting through to schools, 90% was getting through. . .so scrutiny turned 20% into 90%. More effective than doubling aid and doubling it again (p. 150).

A seemingly simplistic solution for an apparently intractable problem, but nevertheless an illustration of the power of mere transparency. But our new transparency is much more than that. It seeks access to progress and the processes (details) that accompany it. To move beyond mere transparency, we have to work on the conditions under which transparency can be used simultaneously for both improvement and accountability. We know that people will cover up and not report problems if the culture punishes them. So, one thing we need to work on is developing cultures in which it is normal to experience problems and solve them as they occur—exactly what the effective organizations we have been discussing do. In other words, effective cultures embrace transparency and the use of data as a core part of their work.

Another reason why transparency rules is that in all cases of successful change, transparent data are used as a tool for improvement. You can't achieve better results without establishing mechanisms for open data collection and use. The solutions to perplexing problems of improving large organizations on a continuous basis are too nuanced and too contingent on precision under dynamic conditions for them to be discovered by individuals working in isolation. Transparency and the use of data on performance and practice can serve as powerful tools for improvement.

A further reason that transparency rules is that the credibility and long-term survival of organizations are dependent on public confidence. Call this external accountability. My colleagues and I have found that as leaders (principals and teachers) get better at using transparent data, two powerful outcomes transpire. These leaders start to positively value data on how well they are doing—with regard to successes and problems alike. They look forward to receiving data and learn to seek data that help them and that show them and others what is being accomplished. The second outcome is that they become more literate in assessment. They are able to explain themselves better. They become more comfortable entering conversations and debates on the meaning of the data and are able to hold their own when it comes to the interpretation and misinterpretation of information. They become both more technically and more politically astute.

In his fable *The Three Signs of a Miserable Job*, Lencioni (2007) offers three ideas for avoiding the first sign of a miserable job, which he labels "immeasurement": "(1) employees need to be able to gauge their progress and level of contribution for themselves; (2) they cannot be fulfilled in their work if their success depends on the opinions or whims of another person, no matter how benevolent that person may be; and (3) without a tangible means for assessing success or failure, motivation eventually deteriorates as people see themselves as unable to control their own fate" (p. 222).

Lencioni argues, as I have done in this book, that people need to be able to compare themselves with themselves over time to assess their progress in achieving important personal and organizational goals. They can't do this without clear transparency showing the causal relationship between practice and results, which enables them to make corrections as they go. No doubt you are dying to know the other two signs of misery at the workplace. One is anonymity (being treated as a nonentity, which represents a violation of Secret One), and the other is irrelevance (the work is seen as unimportant to the supervisor and peers, which violates secrets two and four, connect peers with purpose and learning is the work).

Transparency rules, then, because it is both inevitable (especially these days) and essential. When it is used effectively, the positive power of transparency is enormous. One could even say that transparency is a much more effective way of instilling fear (if that is the issue) than are hierarchical, punitive edicts. Collier

(2007) shows that in the absolutely poorest countries, that early transparency is vital to all serious reform efforts.

This is the time to remind you that the secrets work together to serve as checks and balances in bringing out the best in a given secret while suppressing its riskier aspects. Working backward from what we understand about the secrets we've discussed so far, we can say that transparency rules when it is combined with deep learning in context. Transparency and learning in context flourish when capacity building trumps judgmentalism, when peer interaction fosters coherence, and when employees and customers are equally valued. We have, in other words, a tapestry of secrets that serve organizational leaders in their bid to survive and thrive in complex times. Note this secret has to be tempered if you are in a highly judgmental culture when adversaries are looking to pounce on every misstep or perceived weakness.

When you know that transparency is both inevitable and desirable for successful organizations, it becomes far less threatening. The emperor has no clothes, and he doesn't look so bad after all. But there is more and it is astounding.

A Bridge Not Far Enough

In Secret Four I left the reader dangling with the idea that secrets four and five must feed on each other. Never in our history has there been such a cacophony of confusion about learning. Let's start with one of the seemingly simplest breakthrough findings in the history of learning.

Lee Jenkins has spent more than 50 years in education in the US as teacher, principal, superintendent, university professor. He had a growing interest in whether students liked school.

About a decade ago he asked a sample about 3,000 students across the grade level K-12 "how much they loved school" (see Figure 4.3). Later John Hattie dubbed his findings "The Jenkins Curve"(Jenkins, 2019).

The findings show that "kinders" started at 95% enthusiastic about daily schooling and declined to a low point of 37% by grade 9 (and 45% at graduation). In one sense this a superficial finding—why would students like something that is hard work. But the truth is it is boring for many (see the Brookings findings from Anderson and Winthrop (2025) that we reviewed in the Prologue). The other nuanced finding is what does "loving school" actually mean in terms of intrinsic motivation for learning. Jenkins (2019, p. 10) speculates: "The number hovers around 40%. Further questioning reveals, however that

Figure 4.3: Loss of Enthusiasm by Grade Level

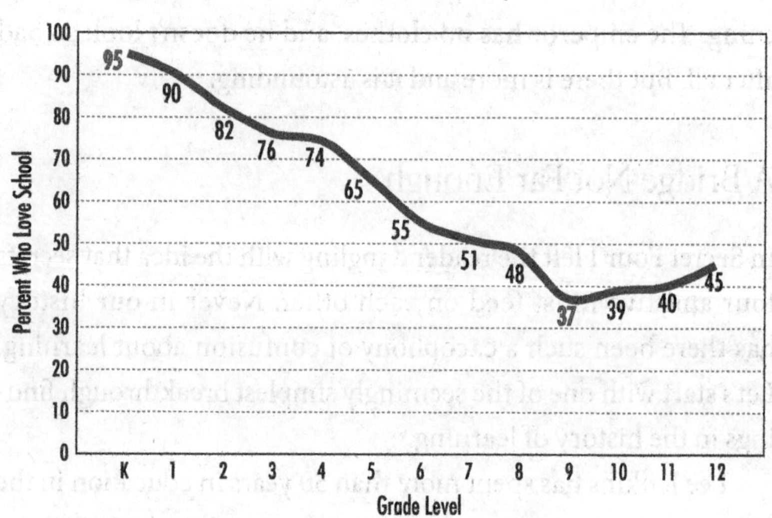

Survey results from 300+ teachers attending L to J seminars between 2009 and 2012. Question was, "What grade level do you teach and what percent of students love school at your grade level?"

only 5–8% of high school students love school learning." This is more or less what Mehta and Fine (2019) found in their large-scale study of *In Search of Deeper Learning*. They did not find much deeper learning in the classrooms but did in the after-schools programs—sports, music, and various clubs. Of course, one implication is why can't academic learning be organized more like the clubs and to a certain extent this has some merit, but we are still left with the question of deeper learning.

The answer that I will take up more fully in Part 3 (along with AI) is more complex than it seems. For now, let me say that we have had two examples that do meet the criteria of genuine learning: Mary Helen's "transcendent learning" and Zaretta Hammond's (2026) *Rebuilding Students' Learning Power* (Secret Four: Learning Is the Work).

The leadership quality is "trust and interact." For universal learning to become embedded you can't pull the strings from a distance. Trust and interact means that you are not following up in order to determine whether workers are *delivering*, but whether you and they are *jointly learning* how to establish and embed the individual and collective capacity to transform the whole system including how to build in continuous improvement. You are trusting and interacting in order *to learn*. When you trust and *interact* you are by definition "proximate to practice." You learn a lot. You have measurably greater impact.

The first five secrets are what we have learned so far over the first quarter of this century. But we need more. There is a crushing need to save society from destruction by offering a new light at the end of a very dark tunnel. I have already offered the newest secret in the Part 1: if a dynamic complex system cannot learn when we leave the future to a collection of bad actors at the top (and we also know that even good actors at the top can no longer make a difference), we might as well consider "turning the system on its head."

6. Secret Six: Systems Learn

*I*n peacetime people get too complacent; in wartime they get killed. No matter how you cut it "War is too important to be left to the generals." Do systems learn? Apparently not very well. Peter Turchin (2023) in *End Times* analyses patterns in the development and decline of societies over the past centuries, concluding that no society has sustained its peak without experiencing a decline within any 200-year period. In 2010, he was asked to use his model to predict the future of the US. His model indicated that the problem occurs when there is surplus of elites, or as he sometimes called them oligarchs. There are limits to the exploitation of the poor. Once it reaches certain limits the system implodes.

The good news (I guess) is that using his model, he predicted in 2010 that "America was in a spiral of social disintegration that would lead to a breakdown in the political order circa 2020" (inside flap of book cover). If we get Secret Six right (along with the other five) maybe we can alter the cycle to 200 years. The first year cannot come soon enough. Secret Six steers in the right direction.

First a precis of what I said in 2008. When the first five secrets are all put into play, the system can and often does learn, but even in the best systems, continuous learning is not guaranteed. Our starting point is that most organizations do *not* learn, and those that do, do not sustain their learning.

I continue to learn from Peter Senge and his team. In 2008 I noted that the first half of Secret Six is to lace the culture with a theory that will travel over time, in which leadership manifests itself at all levels of the organization. Peter Senge (1990) became famous for suggesting that systems thinking was the key to coping with an ever more complex future. Essentially, he said that the number of interdependent factors that existed in the simpler world of the past could be comprehended by a single smart person. Now, he states, the world has become so complex that no one individual can grasp or predict what might happen, because the number of interdependent factors at work and their ramifications are impossible to predict.

Senge's remedy was to increase the capacity to think systemically, in terms of the system as a whole, which would not resolve the problem, but would increase the probability of getting some of it right. An aside, the subsequent practical work of systems thinking has failed to produce leaders who can act in accordance with system thinking. After all, Senge recommended that we develop a body of knowledge and related tools in order "to make the full patterns clearer, and *to help us see how to change them effectively*" (p. 7; italics added). Perhaps the failure to do this is related to the emphasis on system *thinking* rather system *doing*. And possibly it is related to the sheer mega complexity of the 21st-century world.

Currently it is going to take some doing to unravel this secret, but essentially it means being humble and confident at the same time and having the conceptual ideas and practical tools to operate in complex, unpredictable environments. In retrospect I note now: I was right in 2008, but I left the idea of "systems learn" at a too general level. Right idea but not specific enough to be very helpful.

I suppose one advance, albeit perversely, is that we no longer expect leaders to know what they are doing. Pfeffer and Sutton (2000) had nailed this 25 years ago:

1. Everyone expects leaders to matter a lot, even as they have limited actual impact. Leaders need to act as if they are in control, project confidence, and talk about the future, even while recognizing and acknowledging the organizational realities and their own limitations.

2. Because leaders succumb to the same self-enhancement as everyone else, magnified by the adulation they receive, they have a tendency to lose their behavioral inhibitions and behave in destructive ways. They need to avoid this trap and maintain an attitude of wisdom and a healthy dose of modesty.

3. Because the desirability of exercising total control is itself a half-truth, effective leaders must learn when and how to get out of the way and let others make contributions.

4. Leaders often have the most positive impact when they help build systems where a few powerful and magnificently skilled people matter the least. Perhaps the best way to view leadership is as a task of architecting organizational systems, teams, and cultures—as establishing the conditions and preconditions for others to succeed.

Helpful to a certain extent but still not very clear about what we should actually do this time around. When all is said and done, Pfeffer and Sutton are still talking about leaders at or near the top. We are back then to the new model that I outlined in the Part 1: Build the bottom, strengthen the middle, and intrigue the top. We have several specific examples of how to alter the first two levels according to our new theory. Anaheim Union High School District (AUHSD) has been working toward this model for a decade, especially, explicitly and rapidly so in the past two years. We have captured these developments in a new book that will be released in February 2026: Barnett Berry, Michael Matsuda, Michael Fullan, Corwin Press: *The Future of Public Education: A Case Study of AUHSD.*

In another book, Sara Fine, Santiago Rincón-Gallardo, Michael Fullan, *Whole Learners Whole Systems* (March, 2026) we spell out how the middle (five school districts and a county in California) can develop on their own, and *then* focus on relating latterly to other districts, as well as vertically upward (the intrigue part).

A further indication of some shift toward the middle is the new agreement involving ten philanthropic organizations chaired by the Stuart Foundation (our funder) including Gates, Hewlett, and seven others that centers focus on "Youth Thriving Through Learning Fund Investments Prospectus" (YTL, 2025). Dissatisfied with their ad hoc funding of bits of the bottom and middle these philanthropists decided to step back and be more strategic with its investments. Whether this will turn out to be a bottom-middle-top phenomenon remains to be seen, but it is leaning in this direction.

The only way to learn from system change with the "bottom, middle, top" model is through actual examples in action. One must learn from specific examples in order for the learning to be meaningful and usable. My experience in the last 24 months since I first proposed the flipped model is that there is much interest in the possibilities because people now have greater access to what is actually happening on the ground. Top-down models have not been working for some decades. Bottom-middle-up models give people access to the whole system. They even like the new role for the top because: well, people are intrigued by intrigue (sorry).

My take on our new systemness work is that people are attracted to adjacent chunks of the system doing similar new work: schools and districts to their pairing; districts and states to theirs. They like intra-level interaction and learning, but they are also attracted to others doing similar innovative work. The burning question for system change will be: Can we develop examples of radically new systems, while fostering access across systems to affect the whole?

Part 3 will cover designing and constructing such a new system.

PART · 3

Systemness Change and the Future

It's the beginning of 2026 and I have two major contradictory feelings. One is that we are nearing the end of the line. Humans are fighting a losing battle, and the forces for good are not nearly equipped enough to rally and win the day. Some of these significant forces were created by humans but are now no longer within our control. My opposite feeling is that the doomsday scenario can't be inevitable. We have other developments underway that could be positioned in a way that they become more powerful, acquire widespread support, and reverse our fortunes leading to a period of expansive world wide and universe-wide success. I call the former: "In Search of a Future"; the latter I will label: The "Systemness Model in Action."

As we search for a better future the reader will have noticed that up to this point I have not mentioned: "Woke," DEI (Diversity, Equity, Inclusion), and the like. All through my career and many books we have focused on: moral purpose, spirit work, raise the bar and close the gap, universal success, poverty, class, race. There are two reasons why I want to keep an unwavering focus on universal success: One is that it encompasses everyone especially those who are not being successful. Second, most people are not being successful. You have seen the data on purpose and schooling. I think that it is accurate to say that only about 20% of the population is faring well. Therefore, a comprehensive revision of teaching and learning methods is necessary.

A good combination reading for reflecting on what should be the focus for universal success includes: Al-Gharbi (2024) *We Have Never Been Woke*; Kahlenberg (2025) *Class Matters: The Fight to Get Beyond Race Preferences, Reduce Inequality, and Build Real Diversity at America's Colleges*; and Ainscow (2025) *Reforming Education Systems for Inclusion and Equity*. Ainscow is especially good at including most of the elements of system change. Applied directly to our new model (bottom, middle, up), Ainscow spells out the details of the bottom and middle. My reverse emphasis (upward) matters because with the old model people were considering how to specify the lower two levels. With the new model the directional sequence is the reverse. Thus, we can examine success at the lower two levels and then say, "given success at those levels what are the implications for how the top should act differently?"

I should say fundamentally that the future of humanity needs to be radically different than the world we have now. It's *exactly* the time to rebuild when things are falling apart. A little Leonard Cohen: "There is a crack in everything. That's how the light gets in."

The Original Six Secrets

The Big Decline

Turning the System on Its Head

The New Six Secrets

In Search of a Better Future

Systemness in Action

The Future

In Search of a Better Future

The Big Change Model (BCM), AI, and All That

"The most important thing about leadership is to be right at the end of the meeting, not the beginning," David Cote, CEO of Honeywell, 2013.

David Cote: One of my favorite change quotes highlighting that leading change is a process beginning before and continuing throughout implementation and its outcomes.

This chapter has three main parts. I will start with what I call "The Big Change Model" or BCM. Second, we will finally catch up with what is undoubtedly the biggest elephant in the room: Artificial Intelligence. Third, I consider the future, which at this time must be the most unpredictable since post-World War II. When there are cracks in a big edifice crumbling and re-building represents a momentous building opportunity.

The Big Change Model (BCM)

The following figure names the main components of our full working model. The core two—Well-being and Learning—are at the center of purpose and development, The column on the left is "Change Management." The right-side column is "Digital Management."

The core purpose of the work is to increase and integrate "well-being and learning." The means of doing this is to continuously develop the capacity to "manage change and digital factors and issues" during what we can call the furious "dynamic complexity" of conditions that increasingly characterize today's world.

The *Six Secrets of Change* helps us to contend with what I have called the "stuck" nature of where we are. We can accomplish a great deal by mobilizing and building on this knowledge through purposeful action. Ironically it may be comparatively easier to carve out new "systemness change" with the "bottom-middle-top" model under the current helter-skelter times we live in than to organize a more top-down strategy (which doesn't work under any conditions).

My purpose in this chapter is to present a systemness framework that we are currently developing and using—a model that is amenable to a variety of systems around the world. We hope that these ideas will be used and further developed by many others globally. With respect to our main summary model (Figure 5.1) I have already addressed the center of the diagram, especially concerning the complex relationship between Well-being and Learning. The vast majority of what we know and use in education about system change turns out to be somewhat superficial

Figure 5.1: Scope of Secrets for System Transformation

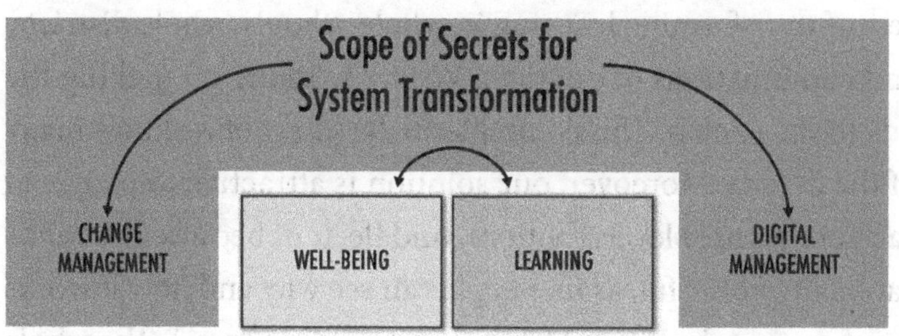

because we have not gone deeply enough in order to integrate "Well-being and Learning." We saw, especially with Immordino-Yang (2025), and Zaretta Hammond (2026), that recent advances in neuroscience have enabled us to pinpoint the dynamic between the emotional and cognitive parts of the brain, buttressed by social factors (working with others). When these core elements interact, they enhance cognitive functioning and improve performance in relationships and tasks involving problem-solving, adaptation, and development in complex situations.

One could speculate that such a process is so complex that it is not available to most of us. Given recent developments (exemplified by Immordino-Yang and Hammond), this inaccessibility may no longer be true. It is independent from IQ; it is about the whole brain. And it is possible that almost all of us can come to understand how it works. Currently in Anaheim a range of high poverty, ethnically diverse students are learning how to focus on their "purpose of learning" (which I have said is wanting for some 80% of students all around the world). They are engaged in an individual and collective enterprise to develop from their current lack of clear purpose (the "here and now") to a "transcendent purpose" ("the then and thereafter").

We now have the details with respect to the comprehensive process of transforming learning in whole schools, whole districts, and combinations of districts. We are working on making the link to state policy. This is complex to be sure, but we know many of the details. Moreover, our solution is attractive to people at each of the three levels (bottom, middle, top) because it is motivationally powerful, as in, people can see why and how it works (see for example, Berry, Matsuda, & Fullan, in press). The whole thing is desperately needed because system quality is in such a sorry state! My colleague Barnett Berry and I have made a small contribution to this direction that has been embraced by the state (see https://edsource.org/?p=743262).

What needs further development are the enabling factors at all levels that could get us to this new destination. Enter the other two parts of our BCM: Change Management and Digital Management in the service of well-being and learning.

Change Management

We know a lot here but unfortunately there is a good degree of superficiality. Micklethwait and Wooldridge (1996) remind us that leadership advice is often too abstract, and that policymakers impose ideas without taking into account local context and are vulnerable to adopting quick fixes. They note that "the fundamental flaw in most innovators strategies is that they focus on their innovations, on what they are trying to do—rather than trying to understand how the larger culture, structures and norms will react to their efforts" (p. 26). In other words, they fail to take into account local context.

In my own analyses of managing change processes I have been consistent in trying to get at alternative ways of managing change. In *Leading in a Culture of Change, 2nd Edition*, I noted that we need to frame the new work as a "learning problem not an execution problem." I offered nine strategies for becoming change savvy:

1. Be right at the end of the meeting.

2. Relationships first (avoid too fast, too slow).

3. Acknowledge the implementation dip.

4. Accelerate as you go.

5. Beware of fat plans.

6. Behaviors before beliefs.

7. Communication during implementation is paramount.

8. Excitement prior to implementation is fragile.

9. Become a lead learner (Fullan, 2020, p. 46).

In *Nuance* (Fullan, 2019), I broke the change process into three broad parts:

1. Jointly determine change.
2. Adaptability: Learn and lead in equal measures (during implementation).
3. Culture-based accountability: Trust and interact.

All of this focuses on managing the change process without which any given change would go nowhere (or worse still—go badly).

The danger of major change going badly is confirmed in spades when it comes to digital transformation (AI). Budzier, Gottschalk, Thuesen, and Lanng (2025) advice for managing change which they call "Seven Levers" in their book, *Intelligent Change*. Their seven are remarkably compatible to mine. I summarize them here as a list of factors, and then in a separate box I provide the full explanation because the details are key. (Note, we will meet these authors again shortly as they report on how they apply this thinking to digital transformation.)

Seven Levers for Success

1. A clear reason for change

2. Defined approach to managing change

3. Early involvement of users

4. Management ownership

5. Effective communication

6. Effective training

7. Trust-based relationships (Budzier et al., 2025, pp. 38, 39).

The full explanation of these Seven Levers is provided here.

1. *A clear reason for change*

Very few organizations will risk the time, effort, and cost of a digital transformation for no reason at all. There will almost always be a reason behind the transformation. How important is it for the organization and management to make the reasons for change clear and relatable?

2. *Defined approach to managing change*

A transformation is a significant undertaking. Beginning a transformation without having planned and clarified the precise approach for managing change down to the last detail. . .What level of planning change will benefit the implementation? What should a good plan look like, and can you do too much planning?

3. *Early involvement of users*

Often the people in charge of implementing a digital transformation are programmers and designers who will never be the end users. . .But do programmers and users? How vital are end users in designing and testing processes, and systems? What should involvement look like, and how early be users involved?

4. *Management ownership*

Management contains several groups with different levels of authority and responsibility: top, middle, and frontline. . ..What does taking ownership of change look like?

5. *Effective communication*

There needs to be communication for management, stakeholders, and end users to cooperate. Change cannot happen without active and deliberate communication. What needs to be considered for this communication to be effective?

6. *Effective training*

A lot of work goes into developing and implementing new systems. However, this effort is wasted if end users do not understand how these systems work. What can be done to ensure that the training is effective, and how early in the life cycle of the transformation as a whole should training be considered?

7. *Trust-based relationships*

　　People make or break change. This lever is about establishing and maintaining productive relationships between end users and stakeholders . . . Having strong relationships based on trust of end users and stakeholders affects success of the transformation. What factors build this trust in the project (Budzier et al., 2025, pp. 38–39).

In summary, effective change management is essential and often represents the most challenging aspect of the overall change process. It is surprising how many leaders don't think of change management as a process; they just think of the content of the change.

Applied AI

We move now to applied AI—probably to the biggest change that humanity has ever faced—certainly in terms of its ubiquity and capacity to affect every aspect of our lives—the innovation that knows no limits: Artificial Intelligence and its Generative cousins (Generative and General Intelligence—see the Box summary I provided in Part 2 from Schmidt & Xu, 2025).

　　I don't blame those who either go full fledge into AI or decide to do nothing and wait and see because things are going a mile a minute and will be outdated by the time you finish your first month of use. The situation does represent a true dilemma. If you decide to take a pass on AI while it goes wild, you may very well be left out in a way that affects you adversely. If you jump in you won't be able figure out how to use AI. I'll do my best to consider where we are and why it is necessary to get involved early i.e., *now*, realizing that no one can predict where we might end up. On balance I say get involved with AI but do so as a self-disclosed learner building your capacity as you go with *systemness* (as we define it) as your *driver*. I will provide two excellent examples shortly.

The biggest indicator that there is something to worry about is that those who helped create AI are the ones who are most worried about the future of where AI will end up—or more precisely where humans will end up. Start with this mindset. *Nobody knows where AI is going, and if big tech, for example say they do, don't believe them.* Put another way, as I will explain shortly AI is inevitable and your best bet is to become a critical consumer. Or as Andy Hargreaves and I have put it, if something is inevitable you should learn how to "move toward the danger" (see the examples later in this section).

We (our team) have followed AI development closely for the past five years. The biggest "dirty little secret" is that AI could result in the extinction of humanity. One of the founders of neural networks AI is Geoffrey Hinton, a Professor at University of Toronto who won the Turing Award in Canada in 2018 (along with Bengio and Yann LeCun). In 2013, he joined Google, eventually becoming part of the team that brought AI, as we know it, into the public domain. He left Google in 2023 due to concerns about artificial intelligence and has served as a prominent spokesperson addressing potential risks associated with AI over the past five years.

One of Hinton's colleagues, Yoshua Bengio, drew a similar conclusion: Yoshua Bengio's May 25, 2025, 16:05 minute Ted

Talk: "The catastrophic risks of AI—and a safer path." Bengio had become an ardent critic of the growth of AI once he realized what they had produced. On October 28, 2023, he had written an Op-Ed in the *Globe and Mail*:

> "I must humbly admit that it was only this year as I studied Open AI's Large Language Model (LLM) Chat/GPT. . .that I realized at an emotional level the magnitude of the risks associated with unbridled advances in AI."

In other words, those closest to AI development are among its biggest worriers. They are telling us that forces are too strong, too hidden, too powerful to contend with. In any case, the genie is out of the bottle, and there are wildly different scenarios emerging. Let's consider three of the most recent: Karen Hao's *Empire of AI*; Reid Hoffman and Greg Beato's *Superagency*; and Ezra Klein and Derek Thompson's *Abundance*.

Karen Hao (2025) is an investigative reporter who dug deep and relentlessly over the past five years to produce a disturbing story in *Empire of AI: Inside the Reckless Race for Total Domination*. She unpacked the story of Sam Altman (CEO of Open AI) and others who have relentlessly pursued the development of AI, which they frequently stated was for the good of humanity (self-deception is not unknown among big innovators). The fact is, there is no reason *to assume* that AI will end up on the plus side of humanity. Here are some of the counter indicators:

> [Feedback from an employee] "How do you reconcile the desire to grow together through crisis with a frustrating lack of transparency" (Hao, p. 5). (Remember our 5th secret:

Transparency Rules.) The mission statement for Open AI was to develop "the most powerful form of AI ever seen, not for the financial gain of shareholders but for the benefit of humanity" (p. 13). Hao concludes: "Over the next four years Open AI became everything it said it would not be."

"It triggered the very race to the bottom that it has warned about, massively accelerating the technology's commercialization and deployment without shoring up its harmful flaws or dangerous ways that it could amplify and exploit the fault lines in our society" (p. 14). Says Hao, "over the years I have found only one metaphor that encapsulates the nature of what these AI power players are: empires" (p. 16). The current result is that "every tech giant is racing to out scale one another" (p. 17). In September 2024 (less than a year ago as I write this) Altman declared in a post: "the Intelligence Age characterized by massive prosperity" would soon be upon us with superintelligence perhaps arriving as soon as in "a few thousand days" (p. 19). Hao's take on this story of the empire is: "It would reveal just how much the quest for dominance of that technology, already restructuring society and terra forming our earth— ultimately rests on the polarized values, clashing egos, and messy humanity of a small handful of fallible people" (p. 45).

You can read the other 400 pages of the Empire's saga but let's conclude. How can you join an empire that flagrantly runs roughshod over every one of our six secrets? Hao speaks time and again of "the overwhelming homogeneity of the people building and shaping such a consequential technology" (p. 53). Despite all this power, the mission of AI led by the big players remains vague (so vague that it "can be interpreted and re-interpreted" (p. 400)). Eventually Altman concluded: "How did we get to the doorstep of the next leap in prosperity?" (p. 405).

By contrast Hoffman and Beato's (2025) *Superagency: What Could Possibly Go Right with Our AI Future.* Hoffman is a venture capitalist, Founder of LinkedIn among many other venture capitalists. Obviously self-interested as an entrepreneur. Yes, I have a major self-interest he states but "I want to see it succeed exactly because I believe it can have profoundly positive impacts on humanity" (p. xvi). As skeptical as we should be, Hoffman and Beato AI take the position that AI should be designed for "human agency" (p. 229). They take the position that we need "to envision *what could possibly go right*" (p. 230, their italics).

The third big treatment of AI is Klein and Thompson's (2025) *Abundance.* Their main analysis is that society has become pre-occupied by a "scarcity mindset" that is embedded in our political and regulatory structures, and that instead we should develop an "abundance mindset" using technology and innovation.

The general rule about AI is don't look for direct answers to complex questions, rather use it to probe further into issues (i.e., AI is only as good as the prompts you use). In the meantime the techno-optimists have a huge advantage, so it's *caveat emptor.* Still, the advice is you need to be a player.

Be Critical Consumer of AI

A huge problem is that grass roots users of AI—students, parents, and educators, for example—are playing into the hands of AI advocates through the ubiquitous use of AI promoted by policymakers and commercial companies. Here's how it works.

Policymakers do their part. It's cool to be ahead of the pack. The US's plan July 2025—this very month of am writing released its 24-page AI manifesto appropriately called: Winning the Race: America's Action Plan. Its first line is: "Today, a new frontier of scientific discovery, defined by transformative technologies, such as Artificial Intelligence. . ." There are three pillars to the Plan titled: "Accelerate AI Innovation; Build America's AI Infrastructure; and Lead in International AI Diplomacy and Security."

Alex Kotran and Christian Pinedo (2025) of aiEdu give us plenty to worry about in their essay "With 'The American AI Action Plan' we're Officially in a global race for AI readiness." They first warn: "AI Readiness isn't just about employability. It's about helping young people navigate a world where AI is shaping how they learn, connect, form relationships, consume media, and make sense of what's real." It's a mistake they say to teach AI readiness only as a technical or career skill. To be successful Kotran and Pinedo argue: "AI must be developmentally grounded, contextually literate, and civically engaging." They then question whether "speed" is a right driver. They define AI Readiness as "AI literacy *along with complementary skills such as critical thinking, problem solving, and collaboration*" (italics in original).

The US plan states, "Winning the AI race will usher in a new golden age of human flourishing, economic competitiveness, and national security for the American people." Then Kotran and Pinedo provide the punchline: "Speed matters; but in education speed without strategy leads to churn What's urgent isn't just how fast we move, but whether we're moving toward systems that honour student agency."

Kotran and Pinedo conclude by saying we face a test of values:

- Are we centering students' best interests in designing or redesigning education systems?

- Are we giving educators on the front line the resources they need?

- Are we building for scale and impact, or just for press ops and ribbon cutting?

- Are we preparing students to become AI users, or to leverage their own human advantage and lead us into the future?

They conclude:

> "Big ideas can't by themselves change complex human systems. People do. And they require steady, principled, collaborative work."

Go back to the Big Change Model that introduced this chapter: Well-being, Learning, Change Management, Digital Management. Ask yourself are we going about AI in a way that is likely to be successful?

In the meantime, commercial firms are building shiny new AI technologies that are attractive, easy to use, and contain a wealth of content information. In our terms the well-being and deep learning elements end up being shallow. It's like the old baseball saying: "It's like being born on third base [the privileged have a head start] and thinking you hit a triple!"

The irony is that there *is* a more productive pathway: if you combine "change management" and "managing digital" with a focus on fostering "well-being and learning" you check all the right boxes for systemness as our two examples will show—it is way more engaging and productive. But in the AI, frenzy people are not checking any boxes. Most are being "swept along" at a breathtaking pace.

I have painted a picture of extreme doubt whether the present forces can result in success. Despite the odds I still recommend we go for it including *the ubiquitous use of technology*. Why? Because you will be worse off if you ignore AI. Let's first discuss what is likely to happen—factors favoring failure. Then we can consider what success looks like and how to get it, which is not as hard as it might sound. Hint, it involves "change management," and what we have been learning about the natural attraction of "systemness in action" with the system forces reversed from top-down to bottom-up (don't misinterpret the latter—all levels are engaged in the new bottom-up model).

The Allure and Price of Superficiality

It would be nice if the only price we need to pay is superficiality. There are two problems: One is that Artificial Generative/General Intelligence can be used with students and teachers with very little significant learning. The other is that it is used without any teacher at all: that advanced AGI evolves to bypass humans altogether on all matters (Bengio's Absolute Catastrophic Fear (Bengio, TED Talk)).

In both cases (AI with or without teachers) there can be a significant drop in the brain development of students (and teachers for that matter). A recent study at MIT raised the question "Does ChatGPT harm critical thinking abilities?" (Chow, 2025). The study divided 54 subjects—18- to 39-year-olds—into three groups asking them to write several SAT essays using OpenAI's ChatGPT, Google's search engine, or nothing at all. The researchers used an EEG (electroencephalogram) to record the writers' brain activity in 32 regions of the brain. They found that of the three groups, ChatGPT users had the lowest brain engagement and consistently "underperformed" at neural, linguistic, and behavior levels. Over the course of several months, Chat-GPT users got lazier with each subsequent essay, often resorting to copy-and-paste by the end of the study.

In another study an MIT researchers asked students to write essays using AI. Two English teachers who rated the essays called them "soulless." The researcher observed that it was more like, "just give me the essay, refine this sentence, edit it, and I'm done."

The next group—called the brain only group—showed the highest neural connectivity, especially in alpha, theta, and delta bands, which are associated with creativity, ideation, memory load, and semantics.

Another study from Harvard (2025) found that AI made people more productive but less motivated to learn. "Motivation dips and boredom grows," say the Harvard researchers. We need caution here. All of this is early work that has not yet been tested rigorously. In the meantime, AI spreads with headlines such as: "No teachers, just AI: Arizona approves bold new charter school." And "AI driven education founded in Texas and coming to a school near you." Shortly I will present two positive cases in large school systems that we work with. The results have great depth, impacting the growth and development of the brain. This better learning requires "proximity and specifics" but is not that difficult partly because the work is absorbingly motivational, and most students are swept up by the learning individually and with others. Their brains made them do it so to speak.

As we approach what is called "Superintelligence" it is a whole new ballgame (the Economist devoted their Summer 2025 issue to the topic). The prediction is that in a few years AI will be better than the average human being at all cognitive tasks (one wonders who is going to benefit from this). By 2028, speculation is that AI will be overseeing their own improvement.

In their feature article, Briefing The race for AGI, the Economist note "it is unusual for the innovators to be the ones panicking." Superintelligence "means an AI so smart no human can understand it." Geoffry Hinton, the AI pioneer, argues that there is a 10–20% chance that the technology will end in human extinction (Economist, Summer 2025, p. 15). Yoshua Bengio puts the risk at the high end. Nate Soares and Eliezer Soares will soon publish a book: "if anyone builds it everyone dies." Soon we won't know in advance what AI might produce because it won't ask anyone for permission—it will just act.

The MIT study had a small sample size N = 54 (with only 18 in the follow-up). It involved only essay writing (a narrow task). It was not peer reviewed. But intuitively we should be worried. The biggest danger I think is that students will take the easy way out (superficial AI) because the world is so extremely vexed. They don't know where to start and have no reason to believe anyone in particular. Many jurisdictions readily embrace AI as the latest way "to be cutting edge." Superficiality of learning is likely to be the outcome.

It is ironic that the price of allowing machines to go more deeply may be accompanied by humans becoming more shallow.

But we do have some hope. We have been working with two large school systems that are having great success, both of which are heavily invested in Generative AI—driven in both cases by *human learning*. These two large systems are out and out successes with deep learning. Let's look at each in turn in terms of: how and why did they embrace and *use* technology to go all the way?

Ottawa Catholic School Board (OCSB)

OCSB is located on the border between Ontario and Quebec. It serves roughly 49,000 students in 87 schools across Ottawa. Mainly middle class in origins, Ottawa Catholic became increasingly diverse enabling schools to become dynamic incorporating issues connected to racial justice, LGBTQ+ rights, and First Nations people as these issues became more salient. They became one of our "New Pedagogies for Deep Learning" (NPDL) districts (Fullan et al., 2018).

In 2023, we commissioned Sarah Fine and Jal Mehta (of *In Search of Deep Learning* fame—Mehta & Fine, 2019) to conduct a case study of Ottawa as a "system-wide" case. They were skeptical. In their wider search, they have found no examples of school-wide success let alone large district-wide transformation. We and the district gave them carte-blanche to examine the system as closely as they could. They were still doubtful but each of them on separate trips studied the schools, observed classrooms, and interviewed a range of students, teachers, and others. In the end, two years later they produced their report: Fine and Mehta (2024): "A Big Tent Strategy for System-Wide

Transformation: Seeking Deep Learning in Ottawa." The report shows widespread deep, shared use of AI across the whole system (some 87 schools).

In what seems like ancient history now, AI entered the scene November 30, 2022, "big time" when ChatGPT was released (seemingly out of the blue). Almost everyone was skeptical. Like most of the world, The Director of Education (as the Superintendents are called in Ontario) Tom D'Amico approached it in his normal way. Tom and the members of OCSB already knew quite a bit about "the secrets of change" in their work having worked with us over the previous decade. The OCSB leaders drew on one of our original secrets that Andy Hargreaves and I had long embraced: "if something big is going to get you, you might as well move towards the danger." D'Amico and crowd did the normal thing (for them): they jointly mobilized—all constituencies to help figure out how best to approach AI.

OCSB have accomplished a great deal through their "big tent" deliberations. In October 2025, Tom D'Amico and his team reviewed their progress and outlined the key actions that led to their current status.

The following diagram depicts what OCSB did in these first three years (what seems in retrospect to be an incredibly brief period). OCSB leaders recognized that AI was powerful, developing at incredible speed, and unknown to most teachers and students. They treated it as any powerful, complex change where large numbers are involved (87 schools, 53,000 students).

They decided that AI to some extent was inevitable and that it would be processed as any large innovation: reduce judgmentalism, focus on capacity building, use peers to teach and support peers, and build out a short and deliberate process. In this case three years: a year of learning, a year of initial implementation, and a year of scale, refinement, and evaluation (see Figure 5.2).

If you look closely you will see that they used "The Six Secrets."

OCSB immersed themselves in an incredible number of AI experiences. As was normal for them they saw this "exposure" to AI as experimental. They knew that no one else knew what they were going to end up with, so that they figured they had to "learn by doing." They had students, teachers, and administrators try things as front end familiarity experiments: 2,000 staff with over 8,000 chatbots (spaces); 3,000 staff with over 143,000 uses with feedback, creating curriculum, inspecting writing, and 2,500 staff with over 10,000 quizzes (including a question: "What is AI anyway?").

They had some guideposts such as the 6Cs: Character/Compassion, Citizenship, Communication, Collaboration, Creativity, and Critical Thinking. They knew that these Cs had to

Figure 5.2: OCSB AI Implementation

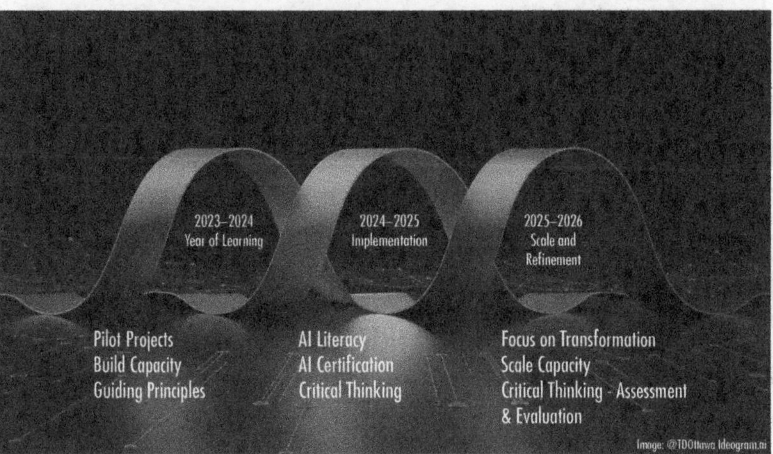

Source: Generated with AI using Ideogram.

be underpinned by well-being, and new pedagogy. They did not insist that all Cs had to be pursued at once. They fixed on critical thinking, and creativity early. They developed exemplary lessons, blank lesson templates, sharing of lesson templates, five reasons why critical thinking skills were important in the age of AI. With all this in the first two years, it was easy to get agreement in the third year that "every school must include the global competency of critical thinking in the age of AI as part of their school improvement plan."

It was also easy to get agreement on creativity and entrepreneurialism, which the students and teachers explored with local businesses and indigenous language learning in the region. In the third-year students translated their math activities into 99 different languages across grades 4–8.

They compared Generation Z (1997–2012) with Generation Alpha (2012–2025) with the observation:

"Let's not make the mistakes with this generation that we made with the last. Digital Natives does not mean they don't need guidance and instruction on the ethical use of technology" (D'Amico, 2025).

When D'Amico recently reflected on what worked well he focused on five things. See Figure 5.3.

"Start with pedagogy not technology" seems particularly apropos given the themes of our secrets! In a final thought about "Where are we going in 2026 onward," D'Amico was crystal clear: "Move from a focus on the tools to a focus on the outcomes" (D'Amico, personal communication, 2025).

Figure 5.3: OCSB Implementation Results: What Worked Well

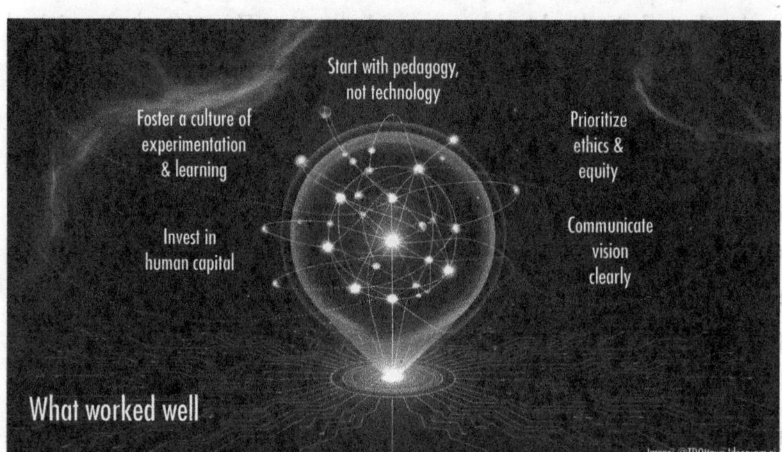

Source: Generated with AI using Ideogram.

The lessons are clear. First, to a certain extent institutions need a well-being/learning foundation. As they are developing this pedagogical readiness they can move into AI development, first in order to get familiar with AI readiness. It should be exploratory and developmental, not prematurely judgmental (people need time to develop new skills and application). As initial learning accumulates, they can accelerate with both pedagogy and the use of technology moving more quickly as the combination allows.

Tom D'Amico retired in July 2025 and was succeeded by Assistant Superintendent Mary Donaghy. They produced a new five minute "Deep Learning Video" of individual students of all ages commenting on the power of deep learning and digital drivers in concert (see OCSB, Video, 2025).

The next two or three years will be a perfect opportunity to test the staying power of the six secrets as OCSB pursues the AI-learning agenda. Will deep learning continue to "drive" technology with the latter playing a supportive role? I conclude here with one powerful change aphorism that should give you shivers every time you hear it. I have already noted that big tech leaders claim that AI will be good, indeed great for humanity. Here is my change guideline: when advocates of change claim *at the macro level* that a particular change is good for humanity take it with a grain of salt. They can't possibly know whether it will be worthwhile at the *micro level* where they rarely spend much time. If there is one change lesson we have learned via our "Secrets" it is that change stands or falls when it gets to *specific use!*

Politicians often make sweeping promises that rarely translate into effective action. The Six Secrets 2.0 shifts our day-to-day perspective from the vague macro level to the day-to-day world where real change stands or falls. Stated another way it turns the system on its head. We mitigate that possibility by placing more control and leadership at the bottom and middle levels.

All of this is confirmed in detail in Bender and Hanna's book, *The AI Con* (2025), which offers several "preemptive steps" to combat what they call AI Hype.

Still, don't miss the main point. The power of AI guided by human values and skills is the future of prosperity. The main risk is that people might use AI in a shallow way, believing they're gaining knowledge when they're really just scratching the surface. This "allure of modernity" has often been humankind's Achilles heel.

Systemness in Action

Anaheim Union High School District (AUHSD)

We have just published a full book on the evolution and current status of AUHSD (Berry, Matsuda, & Fullan, 2026). I have made reference throughout this book that AUHSD exemplifies the *Six Secrets* in action. In this section I want to do two things: (i) show how AUHSD has naturally incorporated AI into all aspects of systemness model of change and (ii) how it has explicitly positioned itself as a player in the bigger system-wide agenda of transforming secondary schooling as a state-wide phenomenon.

AUHSD has 20 schools with 28,000 students. As a high school district in California it goes from grades 7–12. In a previous publication we asked Superintendent Matsuda to capture the key components of their strategy and journey:

"AUHSD has liberated its students, teachers and families from the wasteful practice of chasing higher test scores to educating students for a purposeful life. The Career

Preparedness Systems Framework (CPSF) is a call to action to fulfill a promise too long deferred—to educate the whole child. . . the CPSF framework is a blueprint for integrating Technical Skills and 21st Century skills to elevate student voice and guide students toward their calling or purpose."

"The vision in AUHSD is that every student will graduate knowing the work that he or she would like to do. . .and the capacity to engage in that work. . .A student's purpose might lead to. . .work after graduation, to community college perhaps combined with work, or to four- year university. Achieving this vision requires knowing the students, their assets and their needs, then providing instructional programs that build on strengths and address gaps. A laser focus on empowering students is found in the District's ubiquitous catch phrase, *Unlimited You*" (Fullan & Quinn, 2024, pp. 52–53).

Later we will review the complete AUHSD agenda as of the end of 2025, with particular emphasis on the increasing prominence of artificial intelligence. Almost 15 years ago, societal reform was the context for what evolved. Street crime and gangs in the city of Anaheim were rampant. In a 12-month period, 2011–2013, seven youth were killed by local police. Newly elected (2010) major Tom Tait set out to reform the city, which included the appointment of Superintendent Mike Matsuda in 2014.

Matsuda established a community reform agenda centered on the vision of "creating a better world through 'Unlimited You.'" Matsuda and team eventually linked up with our team to focus on the "Deep Learning Agenda." They collapsed character and citizenship into compassionate leadership to form the 5Cs, and innovative teaching (see Brazer & Matsuda, 2024, for a full account of Anaheim's original model).

Here I want to return to current AUHSD full model that includes integrating AI as an integral goal. To simplify for a moment AI must evolve: from AI Literacy, to AI Readiness, to AI Integration (the stage that both OCSB and AUHSD are currently at). Remarkably almost everyone was at the pre-literacy stage in 2022.

Let's use Anaheim to illustrate an example of what a "full model" looks like in order to draw certain conclusions that will set us up for the final section on "The Future."

This diagram and all the things that AUHSD has developed and is doing are impressive including expanding interest.

Figure 6.1: Transforming Learning: 8 Interacting Factors for Schools and Systems (Berry et al., 2026)

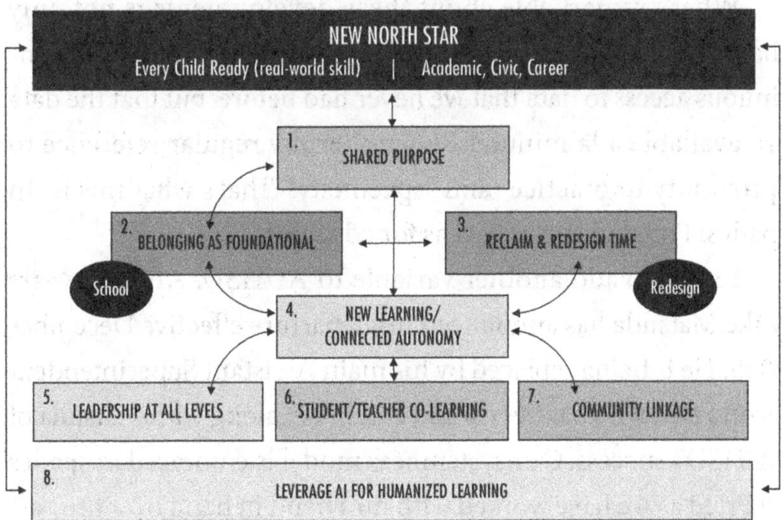

The seemingly little phrase at the bottom: "Leverage AI for Humanized Learning," barely existed five years ago. Now Anaheim places AI as foundational *because it is committed to the transformation of learning.*

And it has all the ingredients: a powerful North Star, a widespread sense of belonging, a change in "structure" and "culture" that supports teachers and students to work together including *time.* Expanding partnership both inside and outside the district to conduct and spread thus work.

AUHSD is partnered with the non-profit technology firm eKadence to develop measurements of the key outcomes (the 5 Cs for example), the nature of key learning strategies, how well graduates are doing in the first year of post-secondary school, and what the community thinks of a variety of ongoing issues. We are also in partnership with eKadence with our chief technologist, Max Drummy working with eKadence on many of these measures.

What's remarkable about these developments is not only that we (including students, teachers, administrators) have continuous access to data that we never had before, but that the data are available à la minute! Remember my regular reference to "proximity to practice" and "specificity." That's what this is. In spades! For students as well as for educators.

I need to add another variable to AUHSD. After 11 years Mike Matsuda has announced his departure effective December 2025. He is being replaced by his main Assistant Superintendent Jaron Fried who has been a chief architect along with Matsuda of AUHSD's success. Our systemness model is embraced in spades by Fried as we have worked with him hand in hand over the past five years and now.

Among other things, AUHSD represents a full-on commitment to the development of *Transcendent Thinking (TT)* (see Figure 6.2). Nothing represents the future of successful learning than refashioning and focusing a powerful *Learning Purpose.* I have already discussed the framing of TT–portrayed here:

We have here the frame of TT. The "black box" of TT includes the core strategies and action that enable students to move from Time 1 (limited sense of purpose) to T2 (transcendent purpose).

The details within this so-called black box are no longer obscure. They are the eight themes in Figure 6.1. Teachers and students (as well as administrators) can describe how they go about the development of T2.

Figure 6.2: Transcendent Thinking: The Key to Kickstarting Learning Transformation

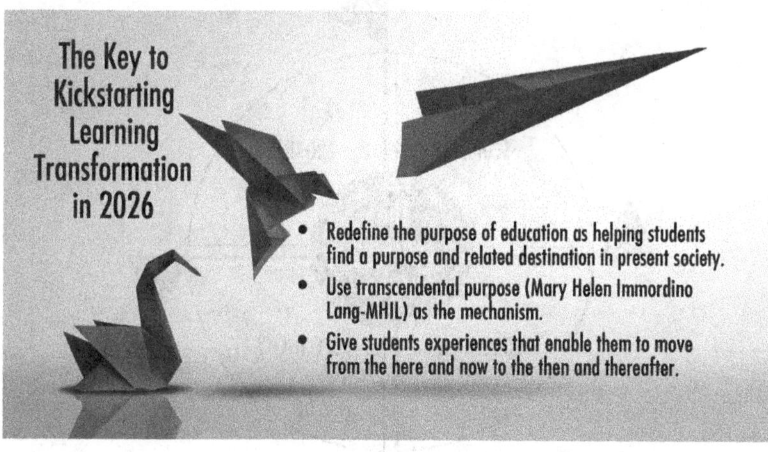

Harnessing Complexity: The Learning Flywheel

We have a powerful new framework that we have developed as part and parcel of being close to action. We refer to it as the "learning flywheel." A perennial problem in working with system transformation is how to implement "complexity." It isn't possible to direct people to carry out complex ideas effectively, even if they are motivated. But when you jointly determine complex innovations, you can develop them in practice through careful guidance and a process that enables insightful new ideas to be embraced "voluntarily" over relatively short time frames (see Figure 6.3). People love it because it works to achieve more deeper and wider learning than ever before.

I have referred several times to "proximity to practice." In the new change paradigm students and teachers work closely

Figure 6.3: The Learning Flywheel

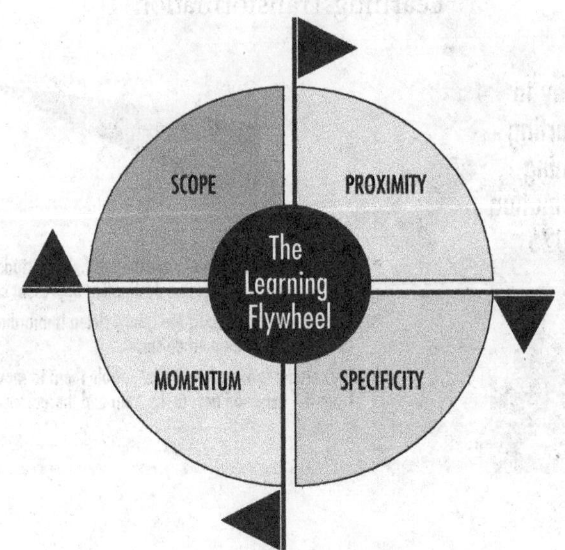

together. For example, the eight factors in Figure 6.1 work together in combinations. It is the *interaction effects* that generate the outcomes.

The full flywheel has four elements: Scope, Proximity, Specificity, and Speed/Momentum. The first requirement is scope. The new work has to have an overriding "purpose" and cover a certain size or proportion of the system. Not just a school, or cluster of schools, or even a district. It needs to be a sizeable chunk of a larger system that starts and feeds the learning as it deepens and widens toward systemness itself.

Second is "proximity to practice"—the day-to-day work. The third requirement—specificity—signifies that there must be something specific and worthwhile to do. Worthwhile nearly always means a degree of complexity (deeper change for example). Note that transparent non-judgmentalism is at play. The combination of the first three factors represents what we call "specificity without imposition." The fourth element—speed/momentum—is also a motivator. In our new age increased speed of change is more prevalent, but it must be integrated with quality and depth. Hence the flywheel in action.

In the new culture (AUHSD, for example) we are constantly developing, experiencing, and describing the new change examples that represent future work and societal life. The transcendent thinking "experiences" are replete with such outcomes. The richness of the examples, their prominence, and the collective nature of learning tied to important publicly valued and demonstrated outcomes further reinforces the learning. At the same time technology (such as eKadence) and learning combine to increase the quality and the speed of change that produces quality learning goals and outcomes.

There is a whole other new domain that I will not elaborate here—that is the increased prominence of career paths, post-secondary, and other related destinations in society that are prominent in the AI world we live in.

The big breakthrough in all this and what makes it truly powerful is that it gives users access to a correlated set of everyday practices that can make a powerful and relatively immediate impact on learning as part and parcel of becoming good "in" and "with" society. This new link to career paths and involvement in business and other aspects of society is becoming increasingly prominent at both the micro (my school and community) and macro (our society) levels. With AI, and lack of purpose in traditional schooling, there is a whole new frontier opening up concerning potential new occupations. Charles Fadel (2024) and his colleagues have opened up and analyzed a new framework of occupational and career dynamics that offers a whole new frontier of dynamic complexity. Only districts that have entered the complex arena of pathways to such a new society have any chance linking their students to viable futures.

For a variety of reasons that I have featured throughout this book we have reached a turning point in our evolution. All things point to some kind of upheaval in this coming decade. Read and consider the final section with a proactive stance. Start figuring out how you can link the Secrets to action in some kind of collective force that relates to your context.

The Original Six Secrets

The Big Decline

Turning the System on Its Head

The New Six Secrets

In Search of a Better Future

Systemness in Action

The Future

The Future

*I*n this final section allow me to speculate and propose what should and could happen for the better, expect change to happen incredibly fast, and don't be surprised if on some days you think it is game over, only to find another day where hope and optimism seem justified. One general piece of advice: make your best secrets known, share widely, and make them as prominent as possible.

This is a wide-ranging story in wider ranging times. Let's consider two main strands as we look to the future: one negative, the other positive. First, there could be continued deterioration if the trends of the last decade continue. People could lose all hope. AI could prevail with superficial learning becoming dominant and intelligence of humans declining.

Second, and by contrast, there could be breakthrough patterns with the right drivers becoming prominent. Good patterns would converge and leverage the system. Included in this latter possibility is that youth and younger could come to the rescue as good developers and implementers of uplifting ideas. This most powerful force for breakthrough transformation could be the hidden potential of young people who have never yet been enabled to rise from their limited starting points. Teachers would be part and parcel of this development partnering with students as the teaching profession finally reaches its potential.

One fundamental problem with the positive scenario is the failure of the teaching profession to flourish. Teachers and the broader society seem to be at a loss today with respect to their role as teachers. In 2004, I wrote an op-ed that I never tried to get published because I thought it might be misinterpreted. It was titled: "Teaching: The Profession that never was." I meant that the profession had never reached its potential because policy initiatives were episodic. At a few junctures in the past 50 years teaching had the potential to become a valued profession in society, but it always fell back. *SSC 2.0* and the case examples we use show the possibility of transformation. The question is why would or could it be different this time? New success (really success for the first time) would require liberating teachers and students into new, more engaging roles. Such a large shift will be hard because people are used to their old roles. They have what sociologist Thorstein Veblen (1857–1929) called a "trained incapacity"—an affinity for what people know and an inability to see beyond it. The transition to a new way where teachers and students—together and with others—begin to learn differently is now underway as we have noted in several places. A better future is hinged on students and teachers working together with external facilitation to help accomplish a new world of learning. So far these new practices have appeared in limited ways. Now we must progress substantially to accelerate this new way of learning. It could go either way—fall into the allure of superficial AI learning or become paired with deep learning to alter the nature of society where humanity and machines combine to create lives of accomplishment never before achieved on any scale.

My colleague Andy Hargreaves recently took up the failed pathway in his lament "High School Change: A Reflective Essay on Three Decades of Frustration, Struggle, and Progress." Hargreaves tries to find a sliver of hope as he observes: "High school change has only failed if it is judged by the overarching criterion of systemwide transformation" (Hargreaves, 2022, p. 1). Hargreaves acknowledges but apparently doesn't believe Seymour Sarason (1990, p. 5—when he originally said in his 1982 famous lament "schools will remain intractable to desired reform, as long as we avoid confronting their existing power relationships"). Hargreaves then quotes Tom Hatch (2022) who queried: "should (high schools be improving what they already do, and undertake everything in their power to make it better, and make it more effective? Or should they be embracing innovation. . .not merely making their existing practice more effective, but transforming that practice and even the nature of their institutions altogether" (from Hargreaves & Shirley, 2009, p. 201).

Hargreaves quotes Hatch: "We need to both improve schools and transform education" (Hatch, 2022, p. 9). Hargreaves then discusses some instances around the world where elements of "both" (transforming practice *and* institutions) have occurred. Frankly there are not such examples on any scale that I can find.

In a nod to Karen Seashore Louis (KSL: another of our colleagues who have fought the battle for secondary school reform for the past 50 years) Hargreaves concludes that with the changes he refers to that "she [KSL] should also feel vindicated that the transformative educational changes for which she has always advocated and that are needed more than ever to protect our future, may finally be within our grasp" (p. 20).

What! "Within our grasp?"! As I have noted there is no evidence of this whatsoever. Rather when it comes to better learning with teachers helping to lead the way we have history of "slip slidin' away." How many transforming the teaching profession commissions do we have to see come and go over a 50-year period to realize that it ain't going to happen through a combination of *general calls for system transformation* along with small scale (at best) examples? We need instead direct assaults on the whole system: Systemness that relentlessly builds the bottom, strengthens the middle, and intrigues the top! Other small-scale work is valuable to a point, but it is not going to carry the day.

I believe we now have an opportunity to seriously pursue the Systemness Model, namely: Turn the system on its head and build what I have called "Systemness in Action." A new teaching profession is needed working jointly with students, linked to AI based on "new learning" of the kind I have described across the secrets.

I can see why the techno-optimists fail to see teachers as valuable because teachers have never evolved from their traditional roles. But the "technos" are confusing what has been with what could be! Even the most ardent technophiles seem to think deep down that humans are essential to augment machine learning. They don't seem to realize that teachers themselves could represent one "abundant possibility" to transform their role to one that focused on the human and techno co-develop with students—one that students would also dearly love to undertake and would be good at. It's a big leap to re-imagine the teaching profession, but what a resource discovery it would be if we augmented machines with a new teaching corps that joined humanity and technology to create a new abundance. This is only but one radical new idea that is generated when you turn the system on its head and "build the bottom." If we don't incorporate a new teaching corps society will fail because technology will fail in the absence of the presence of human ingenuity.

Thus, my best advice is to commit to turning the system on its head and build capacity upward through *"restructuring and reculturing."* Commit to developing teachers and students as co-developers of the learning solution. Even in the best examples this is barely happening—student voice and related input is a poor cousin to fundamental transformation. The irony is that many students and teachers would be open to this new development. Under the right conditions (the Six Secrets in action) we could see rapid movement (go slow to go fast) over the course of this decade. This does not gainsay my analysis that we are deeply "stuck." There are some things and some times when desperate actions present themselves as "worth fighting for"—forces that could make a major difference if positioned and supported properly.

I should stress that the ongoing and current plight of teachers is not the fault of teachers; it is a function of a "culture and system" that has failed to be transformed over the years. For some schools the distance to the change I have been advocating is not so very far judging from the reaction we sometimes get from teachers when they experience the new ways we are exploring ("This is why I came into teaching," they excitedly claim). The new solution will be different in the early and primary years than in middle and secondary schools. In all cases safety and social learning must be established along with time and experiences to develop new learning relative to their role in helping to change society.

In our solution we address head on the old albatross, the grammar of schooling that stultifies transformation (Tyack & Cuban, 1995). In the new paradigm, students participate as co-developers, contributing more than just their ideas. Both experienced members and those new to the environment need to adapt to a fundamentally different culture. All of this is designed to transform "the century and a half-old culture of traditional schooling."

Barnett Berry and I reported some proof of progress in a recent Op-ED in *Ed Source* (Fullan & Berry, 2025: https://edsource.org/?p=743262). The article was entitled: "With a new vision, clear goals and full-buy-in, reinventing high school can happen." We related our own and related developmental work in secondary school re-design, which is being supported by the state and other related entities. In launching the new initiative: "this initiative will fund networks: with the school district and its communities leading the way, inspiring new local and state policies that will sustain their efforts over time." This initiative, also supported by a network of 10 philanthropic organizations, "will fund a network of participating districts to build capacity, identify promising models and share best practices statewide." The pilots can also make progress in measuring engagement and learning using indicators such as agency, course progress, college, career, civic readiness, and graduation.

We don't know whether this initiative will turn out to be a momentum-maker for wider development, but we do know that using "the secrets mindset" with a very specific, on the ground approach that a lot can be accomplished in a short period of time (say two or three years). Our flywheel framework embedded in proximity to practice, liberating student, teacher, and community energy, eventually backed by the state could be the most promising framework for secondary school reform on a large scale. As Prensky (2024, p. 18) said, "real world accomplishment" is a core motivator for young people who want to make a difference.

Restructuring/Reculturing

Over the last 60 years in education our many attempts at *system change* have fallen short because they failed to simultaneously restructure and reculture learning systems: How things are reorganized and how people spend their time, both of which reveal the powerbase of social systems. With respect to restructuring and reculturing, the 8-factor model that we developed incorporates new learning in a deep partnership among students, teachers, administrators, parents, and community (including business partners). Within the model note, for example, elements like "reclaim and redesign time" and "new learning." Honoring such transformation in practice has become extremely difficult because a century and half of "the way we do things around here" has established habits that no longer work in the 21st century. We can change those habits by supporting students and teachers who will rise to the occasion.

The bottom line here is that the transformation to a new (and better culture) needs a concerted effort. At the beginning the innovation needs new kinds of people, but we also need new empathy for veteran teachers who might change. We need more appreciation and respect for their talents as the transformation to a new system takes place. The growing chaos of the existing system makes new fundamental change possible as we give people new experiences that become recognized as potentially desirable, including instances of actually implementation in some parts of the existing system. Our "Learning Flywheel"—focus, proximity, specificity, and speed/momentum—gives additional hope. The transformation can be put in motion more rapidly than we might appreciate: three years rather than never.

All of this helps explain why California's Learning Policy Institute's otherwise terrific "10 Features for High School Re-design" has had such difficulty getting off the ground (see Figure 7.1). It's a good list but it is *not a system!* Our model on page 80 *is a system,* namely a small number of key factors (in this case 8) designed to interact. It is the interaction effects that cause

Figure 7.1: Ten High School Redesign Features
(Hammond et al., 2024)

Ten High School Redesign Features

1. Positive developmental relationships
2. Safe, inclusive school climate
3. Culturally responsive and sustaining teaching
4. Deep learning curriculum
5. Student-centered pedagogy
6. Authentic assessment
7. Well-prepared and well-supported teachers
8. Authentic family engagement
9. Community connections and integrated student supports
10. Shared decision-making and leadership

transformation: new purpose + focused teacher-teacher-student interaction + time + flywheel momentum integrating proximity, specificity, speed, and so on.

We have not been able to overcome what seems to be our birthmark of the one room schoolhouse of how students, teachers, principals, and parents relate to each other. This is why Andy Hargreaves has had 30 years of frustration in trying to develop teacher collaboration, and why our second factor—the change agent role of students—has failed to take except for token moves, or deeper examples that have failed to take hold.

The Role of Youth in Determining Our Future

Young people today are evolutionarily and experientially different than previous generations. According to Prensky (2024) the current generation—the only ones born in the age of the internet—will grow up differently than any previous generations: "The capabilities of these rising humans…will be by 2040, dramatically increased. This new generation will be far more empowered to change things positively in their world." Then taking a page from my book, so to speak, Prensky concludes: "This new generation of humans, suddenly empowered in a new bottom-up way, will begin to make enormous positive change in the world" (p. 9).

Prensky shows how learning can be organized around "real-world accomplishment—the actual demonstration of getting useful things done, and having impact" (p. 38). These new creatures, so to speak, are built differently. At a very early age, unlike their parents, they know something is wrong, and they need to be built to do something about it. They need and are responsive to critical thinking, creativity, and empowerment for real-life accomplishment with positive impact. They want to work with each other and adults who will help them accomplish something worthwhile that they can build on.

Learning projects "need to relate to and involve each person's dreams, interests, uniqueness, talents, skills, and passions" (p. 225). (Think "transcendent thinking.") This is, in fact, *Six C paradise!*

Aside from the mess we are currently experiencing, Prensky provides some significant links to a radically new line of development. He shows how the very young can grow up with five strengths (none of which schools currently cultivate):

1. High enthusiasm

2. Lower stress

3. High imagination

4. Self-knowledge (passionate about a significant problem)

5. Real-world accomplishment (measurable positive impact)

All of this is within the capacity of nearly all young people. I have been linking off and on with Peter Senge for decades. Our current work, along with our team member Dr. Jean Clinton, a Neuroscientist and Child Psychiatrist, goes under the general title of "cultivating the innate systems of intelligence of children." With Peter's permission I quote some excerpts from the draft paper:

"Traditional education often neglects the innate capacity of systems intelligence [of the very young]." Senge and his team highlight practical examples of systems intelligence using feedback loops to resolve conflicts, demonstrating the intuitive nature of this thinking." By weaving systems science into Socio-Emotional Learning (SEL) Senge and team are developing a "transformative educational paradigm that fosters a deeper understanding of interconnectedness and agency in addressing global issues."

Senge et al.'s premise is that:

"We believe children have an in-born capacity to understand interdependence and change. Failing to recognize and develop this capacity constitutes a fundamental shortcoming of the modern education system." Senge and is team are able to extend these themes to macro issues: "Effectively cultivating systems intelligence can provide a foundation for understanding not only self and other but larger social and ecological problems, from global migration and poverty to climate change, and to cultivating a sense of agency in engaging such issues."

Senge states:

"We focus in this paper especially on early learners and primary school because we believe this is the highest leverage strategy, both because of the ease with which young learners take to the types of tools and learning strategies involved and because of the natural fit with the more open and flexible nature of early years schooling."

We have already presented Mary Helen Immordino-Yang's (2025) development of "Transcendent Thinking" applied to the second brain growth spurt of the teen years. One of my sons (Josh Fullan who is in his early 50s) has been working with youth for the past 15 years or so in his company, *Maximum City*. In July 2025, I asked him how much progress was being made in "turning the system on its head" by altering education systems to involver youth in co-building as new future. Here is part of his response:

> "The fact that children play almost no role at all in developing their system thinking or contributing ideas to their school or city systems is not only anti-democratic and anti-human it is anti-proficient. Systems improve with understanding of their interdependence as users by providing relevant feedback in continuous loops.
>
> Our work uses student or youth voice to address this problem in different systems—schools, cities, sporting and cultural events like the upcoming World Cup. The challenge with typical approaches to student voice or youth involvement can be distilled to: 1. Student or youth voice is almost never collected well or meaningfully. 2. If it is collected thoughtfully, it isn't used as an evidence base for positive change. It is not enough to collect it and report on youth involvement; there is a moral obligation to act on it.
>
> Children are invariably capable of more than we think. Yet they do not want to control their education or schooling or even design it on their own, they want to be co-creators or co-pilots with a sense of agency. Teachers sometimes have trouble with this because they don't feel agentic themselves—it

is hard to help others have agency when you don't feel a sense of agency over your own work or life. And schools think student voice means kids taking over the program and the curriculum—not at all" (Josh Fullan, July 30, 2025).

The role of young people is essential in 2026 and following because it can have immediate and long-term impact. What if they are called upon to play a special role in transforming learning? In the indigenous cultures the notion that "the children will bring the medicine" is not farfetched (my thanks to elder Kahontakwas Diane Longboat, Mohawk Nation at Six Nations in Grand River, Ontario, for sharing this observation). More broadly the anxious generation could become the uplifting generation.

Systemness: Change the Way We Think About Change

As for our overall new paradigm, the difference I see now about our work compared to others is that the latter are still trying to figure out how to impact the bottom and middle—whereas we are trying to position the bottom and middle differently as forces for change: To be a wedge to enter and transform the very system as a whole to be an entire new system altogether!

For all the ways I have looked at and thought about the question of "what is a human?" I think there is something different emerging. It may be related to what I referred to earlier as "the uncanny valley," usually defined as "an eerie feeling that humans have when they encounter human-like entities that are almost human but not quite." Several things are happening with new change—the way we experience and react to our current experience as groups of humans. The nature of the six secrets are similar by label, but different by breed.

Interacting with, and as I suggested the inevitability of partnering with, AI is bound to change us, and indeed to change itself. I also considered Repenning and Kieffer's (2025) new book, *There's Got to Be a Better Way*. They refer to "dynamic work design." In their work with organizations they show how many are attracted to the notion of going from "static" to "dynamic systems." All of our best new concepts cannot be easily contained: proximity, specificity, speed, turning the system on its head (unleashing new forces), putting people back in the process (R & K call it connecting the human chain/putting people back in the work), and making new work visible.

It is true that AI has grossly benefitted big tech and those that run it, but even they cannot control it, even less so as AI forms and transforms itself. When I wrote *SSC 1*, prosperity and safety were not even on the agenda.

In sum, my argument is turn the system on its head: Build the bottom, Strengthen the middle, and Intrigue the top. (P.S. I was happy to find out that when co-pilot offered to rephrase this sentence, and I clicked yes, the response was: "there was no safe rephrasing of this advice.") Once you get the hang of the new paradigm, participation flows and new outcomes become evident. Don't waste your time if the top shows no interest in the short run. The gains far outrun the risks when good secrets are your friend.

Nothing proves itself like learning through experience! Learning by doing has never had such poignant meaning!

Just as was we were about to go to press The Brookings Institution published its new major report, January 14 2026: 'A new direction for students in an AI World' (Burns et al., 2026). We are about to help implement this report that nails AI and the future of students, but does not address 'system change'. The Brookings report and The Six secrets of Change 2.0 were made for each other: a chance to transform the future of learning by integrating technology and humanity!

REFERENCES

Ainscow, M. (2025). *Reforming education systems for inclusion & equity*. London: Routledge.

Al-Gharbi, A. (2024). *We have never been woke*. Princeton University Press.

Anderson, J., & Winthrop, R (2025). *The disengaged teen*. New York: Crown.

Barling, J. (2023). *Brave new workplace: Designing productive, healthy, and safe organizations*. Oxford, UK: Oxford University Press.

Berry, B., Matsuda, M., & Fullan, M. (2026). *The future of public education: One districts journey to transform schools and systems*. Thousand Oaks, CA: Corwin Press.

Bishop, R. (2023). *Teaching to the Northeast*. Auckland, NZ: NCCER Press.

Boushey, H. (2019). *Unbound: How inequality restricts our economy and what we can do about it*. Cambridge, MA: Harvard University Press.

Brazer, D., & Matsuda, M. (2023). *Educating for purposeful life.* Harvard Education Press.

Budzier, A, Gottschalck, T., Thuesen, K., & Lanng, A. (2025). *Intelligent change.* John Wiley & Sons.

Burns, M., Winthrop, R., Luther, N., Venetis, E., & Karim, R. (2026). *A new direction for students in an AI world: Prosper, Prepare, Protext.* Brookings.

Chow, A. (2025). *ChatGPT may be eroding critical thinking skills.* TIME June 23.

Cole, P. (2004). *Professional development: A great way to avoid change.* Melbourne: Centre for Strategic Education.

Collier, P. (2007). *The bottom billion: Why the poorest countries are failing and what to do about it.* Oxford: Oxford University Press.

Collins, J. (2001). *Good to great.* New York: HarperCollins.

The Economist. (Summer 2025). *The economics of superintelligence.*

Elmore, R. (2004). *School reform from the inside out.* Cambridge, MA: Harvard University Press.

Fadel, C. (2024). *Education and competencies for the age of AI.* Boston: Center for Curriculum Redesign.

Fadel, C., Black, A., Taylor, A., Slesinski, J., & Dunn K. (2024). *Education for the Age of AI: Why, what & how should students learn for the age of Artificial Intelligence.* Amazon.

Farrington, F., Johnson, D., Allensworth, E., Nagaoka, J., Roderick, M., & Williams Beechum, N. (2012). *Teaching adolescents to become learners*. Chicago: UCHICAGO Consortium on School Research.

Fensterstock, N. (forthcoming). *Tentative title: Graduating students who are good for society and Good in Society*. UCLA.

Fine, S., & Mehta, J. (2024). A "big tent" strategy for system-wide change. New Pedagogies for Deep Learning. https://bit.ly/NPbigtent24

Fine, S., Rincon-Gallardo, S, & Fullan, M. (in press). *Whole learners whole systems*.

Fullan, M. (1993). *Change forces: Probing the depths of education reform*. Routledge.

Fullan, M. (2001). *Leading in a culture of change*. San Francisco: Jossey-Bass.

Fullan, M. (2008). *What's worth fighting for in the principalship*. 2nd ed. New York: Teachers College Press (and Toronto: Ontario Principals' Council).

Fullan, M. (2010). *All systems go*. Thousand Oaks, CA: Corwin Press.

Fullan, M. (2019). *Nuance: Why some leaders succeed and others fail*. Thousand Oaks, CA: Corwin Press.

Fullan, M. (2020). *Leading in a culture of change*. 2nd ed. Jossey-Bass: Wiley.

Fullan, M. (2023). *The principal 2.0*. Hoboken, NJ: Jossey-Bass.

Fullan, M. (2024). 8 steps to revolutionize education. *Education Week*. https://www.edweek.org/leadership/opinion-8-steps-to-revolutionize-education/2024/05

Fullan, M. (2025). *The new meaning of educational change.* 6th ed. New York: Teachers College Press.

Fullan, M., & Edwards, M. (2022). *Spirit work: And the science of collaboration.* Thousand Oaks, CA: Corwin Press.

Fullan, M., & Quinn, J. (2015). *Coherence.* Thousand Oaks, CA: Corwin Press.

Fullan, M., & Quinn, J. (2024). *The drivers.* Thousand Oaks, CA: Corwin Press.

Fullan, M., Quinn, J., & McEachen, J. (2018). *Deep learning: Engage the world change the world.* Corwin.

Fullan, M., & Tinney, J. (2024). Core concepts for system transformation: Leadership Tool Kit. Unpublished. Available at www.m.fullan.ca.

Gawande, A. (2007). *Better: A surgeon's notes on performance.* New York: Metropolitan Books.

Gonzalez, E. (forthcoming). *Human development at the heart: A multi-case study of innovative teaching in a public secondary school district.* UC: Rossier.

Greenberg, M. (2023). *Evidence for social and emotional learning in schools.* CA: Learning Policy Institute.

Hammond, L. D., Hernandez, L., & Jones-Walker, C. (2024). *Redesigning high schools with the learner at the center.* Palo Alto, CA: Learning Policy Institute.

Hammond, Z. (2026). *Rebuilding students' learning power.* Thousand Oaks, CA: Corwin Press.

Hao, K. (2025). *Empire of AI: Inside the reckless race for total domination*. Penguin, Random House, UK.

Hargreaves, A. (2022). High school change: A reflective essay on three decades of frustration, struggle & progress. *Journal of Educational Administration*, 60, pp. 245–261.

Hargreaves, A., & Fullan, M. (2012). *Professional capital*. New York: Teachers College Press.

Hargreaves, A., & Shirley, D. (2009). *The fourth way: The inspiring future for educational change*. Thousand Oaks, CA: Corwin.

Hatch, T. (2022). *The education we need for a future we can't predict*. Teachers College Press.

Hoffman, R., & Beato, G. (2025). *Superagency*. New York: Anchor Equity.

Immordino-Yang, M. H. (2025). Transcendent thinking may boost teen brains. Feb. 2025 Issue, Neuroscience, February Issue.

Isaacson, W. (2017). *Leonardo da Vinci*. New York: Simon & Schuster.

Jenkins, L. (2019). *How to create a perfect school: Maintain students' motivation and love of learning*. LtoJ Press.

Kahlenberg, R. (2025). *Class matters: The Fight beyond race preferences, reduce inequity, and build real diversity at America's Colleges*. UK: Little Brown.

Kirtman, L. (2025). *Shaping the future: Four leadership pivots*. Thousand Oaks, CA: Corwin Press.

Kirtman, L., & Fullan, M. (2016). *Leadership: Key competencies for whole-system change.* Bloomington, IN. Solution Tree.

Klein, E., & Thompson, E. (2025). *Abundance.* Amazon.

Kotran, A., & Pinedo, P. (2025). With 'The American AI Action Plan' we're officially in a global race for AI readiness.

Kuhn, T. (1962). *The structure of scientific revolutions.* University of Chicago Press.

Lencioni, P. (2007). *The three signs of a miserable job.* San Francisco: Jossey-Bass.

Li, F.F (2022). *The world I see.* Flatiron Press.

Liker, J. (2004). *The Toyota way.* New York: McGraw-Hill.

Liker, J., & Meier, D. (2007). *Toyota talent.* New York: McGraw-Hill.

Machiavelli, N. (1992/1532). *The prince.* New York: Collier.

Malin, H. (2018) *Teaching for purpose: Preparing students for lives of meaning.* Cambridge, MA: Harvard University Press.

Martin, R., & Osberg, S. (2015). *Getting beyond better: How social entrepreneurship works.* Boston, MA: Harvard Business School Press.

Mazzucato, M. (2018). *The value of everything: Making and taking in the global economy.* New York: Hatchette Book Group.

Mazzucato, M. (2021). *Mission economy. A moonshot guide to changing capitalism.* New York: Penguin Press.

McGregor, D. (1960). *The human side of enterprise.* New York: McGraw-Hill.

Mehta, J., & Fine, S. (2019). *In search of deeper learning.* Cambridge, MA: Harvard University Press.

Metcalf, H., & Urwick. (2013). *Dynamic administration: The collective papers of Mary Parker Follett.* Martino Fine Books.

Micklethwait, J., & Wooldridge, A. (1996). *The witch doctors: Making sense of management gurus.* New York: Times Business.

Miller, L. (2002). *Lincoln's virtues.* New York: Vintage Books.

Mollick E. (2024). *Co-intelligence: Living and working with AI.* Penguin, Random House.

Morvan, J. (2023). A quest for equity in school mathematics in Ontario: Connecting Black secondary school secondary school experiences and achievement to principal leadership. PhD dissertation, Brock University, Ontario, CA.

Ottawa Catholic School Board. (2025). *Deep learning at the OCSB.* Video Voices from Students, Teachers, Administrators, Author.

OXFAM International. (2025). *Billionaire wealth surges by $ 2 Trillion in 2024.* Author.

Pfeffer, J. (2007). *What were they thinking? Unconventional wisdom about management.* Boston: Harvard Business School Press.

Pfeffer, J., & Sutton, R. I. (2000). *The knowing-doing gap: How smart companies turn knowledge into action.* Boston: Harvard Business School Press.

Pfeffer, J., & Sutton, R. I. (2006). *Hard facts, dangerous half-truths and total nonsense: Profiting from evidence-based management.* Boston: Harvard Business School Press.

Pink, D. (2009). *The surprising truth about what motives us.* New York: Penguin.

Prensky, M. (2024). *Third millennium kids: A hell yes! low stress guide for everyone.* EAI Publishing.

Raworth, K. (2017). *Doughnut economics: 7 ways to think like a 21st century economist.* White River Junction, VT: Chelsea Green Publishing.

Repenning, N., & Kieffer, D. (2025). *There's got to be a better way.* New York: Venture.

Rizzotto, J. (2025). *Shifting the schema of schooling: The introduction of generative regulation theory.* Viterbo University.

Robinson, S. K., & Robinson, K. (2022). *Imagine if. . .Creating a future for us all.* New York. Penguin Books.

Rosenzweig, P. (2007). *The halo effect and eight other business delusions that deceive managers.* New York: Free Press.

Rubin, R. (2003). *In an uncertain world.* New York: Random House.

Sarason, S. (1990). *The predictable failure of education reform.* Jossey-Bass.

Schmidt, E., & Xu, S. (2025). Silicon Valley is drifting out of touch with the rest of America. *New York Times,* Opinion, Guest Essay, August 19, 2025.

Schonert-Reichl, K., Buote, D., Baelen, R., Lovett, J., Al-Khalaf, M., Bourke, K., Galloway, C., Parker, A., & Baghdady, A. (2023). Leveraging the evidence on the relationship between teacher and student well-being learning & teaching: A scoping review and educator and student interviews. Qatar Foundation.

Senge, P. (1990). *The fifth discipline*. New York: Doubleday.

Sheth, J. (2007). *The self-destructive habits of good companies*. Upper Saddle River, NJ: Wharton School Publishing.

Sirota, D., Mischkind, L., & Meltzer, M. (2005). *The enthusiastic employee*. Upper Saddle River, NJ: Wharton School Publishing.

Sisodia, R., Wolfe, D., & Sheth, J. (2007). *Firms of endearment: How world-class companies profit from passion and purpose*. Upper Saddle River, NJ: Wharton School Publishing.

Stacey, R. (1992). *Managing the unknowable*. San Francisco: Wiley.

Stuart Foundation. (2025). *Youth thriving though learning Fund Investment Prospectus*. Author.

Taylor, F. W. (2007). *The principles of scientific management*. Charleston, SC: Biblio Bazaar. (Original work published 1911).

Taylor, W., & LaBarre, P. (2006). *Mavericks at work: Why the most original minds in business win*. New York: Morrow.

Ton, Z. (2023). *The case for good jobs*. Cambridge, MA: Harvard Business Press.

Turchin, P. (2023). *End times: Elites, counter elites and the path of political disintegration*. New York: Penguin Press

Tyack, D., & Cuban, L. (1997). *Tinkering toward Utopia: A century of public-school reform*. Cambridge, MA: Harvard University Press.

US Office of the President. (2025). *Winning the race America's AI Action Plan*. Author.

Welch, J. (2001). *Jack: Straight from the gut*. New York: Warner Business Books.

Wilson, D. S. (2007). *Evolution for everyone*. New York: Delacorte Press.

ACKNOWLEDGMENTS
The Six Secrets of Change 2.0

MICHAEL FULLAN

I am awash with gratitude for the thousands of people who influence and help me work through the mystery of complex change. Most of them are practitioners. The secrets they convey are below the surface but always recognizable once unveiled. The Six Secrets individually and together are compounded so it's somewhat complex. But when you use them in combination they become "sticky." They occur to you spontaneously when you are in the midst of action. Each spontaneous use adds to the lore.

There are too many to thank but here is my quick long list: Eleanor Adam, Michael Barber, Tiffany Bassin, Barnett Berry, Alan Boyle, Miguel Brechner, Davis Campbell, Michael Chechile, Jean Clinton, Tom D'Amico, Stephen de Groot, Ryan Donaghy, Max Drummy, Sara Fine, Mary Jean Gallagher, Avis Glaze, Andy Hargreaves, Terry Jakobsmeier, Babs Kavanaugh, Lyle Kirtman, John Malloy, Mike Matsuda, Dalton McGuinty, Tim Nguyen, Joanne Quinn, Santiago Rincón-Gallardo, Joanna Rizzotto, Pasi Sahlberg, Peter Senge, Brendan Spillane, and Jordan Tinney.

To Jossey-Bass (Wiley) and their editors who sought me out for key publications and second editions as we produced a small library on change leadership. JB editors were consistently creative, responsive, and models of quality production. Thank you!

To my work "family": the ubiquitous Tony Mackay (who wrote the Foreword and acts as my consigliere); Bill Hogarth, who hasn't found a problem that he doesn't want to solve; Sophie Fanelli and the Stuart Foundation, who have funded our work every year for past two decades. SF are true and relentless champions of "systemness change." Great continuing thanks to Claudia Cuttress who over the past three decades produced all the books and media presentations with relentless creativity, speed, and wisdom.

To my family, family: five children (Chris, Maureen, Josh, Bailey, Conor—two of whom work in the same field as me), spouses, and grandchildren who fill the hallways of our frequent get togethers. Finally, all of this is overlayed and underlaid by my wife of 40 years, Wendy—a spark of life, a font of wisdom, playful, and whose battery never wanes.

I could not be luckier. Thank you one and all!

ABOUT THE AUTHOR

MICHAEL FULLAN, ORDER OF CANADA, IS PROFESSOR EMERITUS and Former Dean of OISE, University of Toronto. Working with practitioners, including students, Fullan and his colleagues are immersed in "applied system change" to improve learning for all students. He and his colleagues focus on "improve the bottom, strengthen the middle, and intrigue the top." Four books written in the last two years have captured this groundbreaking work that he calls "Systemness in Action": *The New Meaning of Educational Change, 6th Edition*; *The Future of Public Education* (Berry, Matsuda, Fullan); *Whole Learners, Whole Systems* (Fine, Rincón-Gallardo, Fullan), and his newest one: *The Six Secrets of Change 2.0*.

INDEX